Liverpool '81

Remembering the Riots

Edited by

Diane Frost and Richard Phillips

With new photographs by
**Goff Tinsley, Donnamarie Barnes
and Mike Boyle**

Liverpool University Press

First published 2011
Liverpool University Press
4 Cambridge Street
Liverpool, L69 7ZU

ISBN 978-1-84631-668-5

Set in Calluna with Hypatia display by
Koinonia, Manchester
Printed in the European Union by
Bell and Bain Ltd, Glasgow

Contents

List of Figures

Acknowledgements

Many people have contributed to this book. The generosity of spirit has been both touching and encouraging. First and foremost, we owe a huge debt of gratitude to those who constitute the very core of this book – the interviewees. While we have not been able to use all of the interviews due to constraints of time and space, we would like to thank everyone who contributed, particularly for your willingness to share your memories and experiences of the riots. Without these, there would be no book at all.

We appreciate the commitment shown by Liverpool University Press in commissioning the book and providing funds for the transcription of oral testimonies. We are particularly grateful to Anthony Cond and John Belchem at the Press for their engagement with this project.

Also, we acknowledge the generosity of copyright holders who waived copyright fees and gave permission to reproduce in full previously published pieces: The Institute of Race Relations, who allowed us to quote from *Race & Class*; Taylor & Francis Publishing who allowed us to reproduce the P. J. Waller article (*New Community* 1981–82); Jacquelin Burgesss, who allowed us to reproduce an essay on media coverage of the riots; Mr Linton Kwesi Johnson, who granted permission to reproduce a stanza of his poem 'Mekkin Histri'; and John Benyon for kindly allowing us to reprint material from his 1984 book *Scarman and After*.

For their helpful suggestions and critical insights we are also grateful to Dave Featherstone and Sandra Walklate.

For their valuable assistance with transcription and scanning, we would like to thank Sandra Mather and Suzanne Yee in the Graphics Section at the School of Environmental Sciences, University of Liverpool.

We thank Goff Tinsley for his generosity in allowing use of unseen photographs taken the morning after Sunday night's rioting; John Cornelius for kindly allowing us to reproduce three of his illustrations; and Donnamarie Barnes and Mike Boyle for taking new photographs in the Liverpool 8 area. We regret only being able to use a small number of these.

We would especially like to thank Christine Gibbons (National Museums Liverpool), Derek Murray and Gideon Ben-Tovim, all of whom gave so much time and support throughout the project.

Figure 0.1 'All riot on the night', by John Cornelius,
from *Liverpool 8* (London: John Murray, 1982).

Introduction
Remembering the Riots

In the summer of 1981, disturbances took place in many of Britain's major cities, and these were particularly intense and sustained in Liverpool. A resident of Lodge Lane, in the city's 'Liverpool 8' district, described the scene outside his home on the night of 3rd July.

> Outside, the entire skyline is an angry crimson. Dense banks of black smoke hang threateningly above the rooftops. The silhouette of Tiber Street School, five hundred yards away, is framed by huge tongues of green and lilac flame, licking skyward. Over by the Anglican Cathedral is a colossal blaze, the like of which we've never seen in our lives. By its position, we guess it must be the Rialto building going up. Almost as huge is the conflagration over in Parliament Street where there is a tyre factory and a couple of petrol stations ... Mass looting is taking place. Figures can be seen silhouetted against blazing shops, wheeling loaded shopping trolleys ... the view is like a Hieronymus Bosch painting of Hell.[1]

This was the first of four nights of rioting, followed by six weeks of aftershocks, which were to leave a strong mark on the city and beyond. These events were sparked when a black motorcyclist was arrested by the police. A crowd gathered and stoned the police while the motorcyclist made his escape. When police reinforcements arrived, a battle ensued. After four days of riots, 150 buildings had been burnt down and countless shops looted, while 258 police officers needed hospital treatment and 160 people had been arrested.[2] Six weeks later, when the disturbances died down, 781 police officers had been injured and 214 police vehicles damaged, according to the Chief Constable's Report to the Merseyside Police Committee ('Public Disorder on Merseyside', July–August 1981). Injuries were of course also sustained by rioters, and though few of these were officially recorded some came to public attention, with powerful consequences. When police vehicles were used to disperse groups of rioters, one young man was knocked down and killed, provoking another series of clashes.

These events are vividly remembered. The thirtieth anniversary of the Liverpool riots presents an opportunity to ask how they have been remembered and why, and to trace their impacts: what has become of the people and places most directly affected by the riots? And what of their wider implications?

This book does two things. First, it draws together the stories and memories of the riots from the perspective of those who were most directly affected. Second, it traces the impacts of these events, both locally and nationally. The book explores the memory and significance of the riots from those who were involved, including residents of Liverpool 8 where the rioting took place; community workers and leaders; photographers and writers; those who took to the streets; and others whom they confronted in the police lines. Piecing together experiences and memories of the riots and their aftermath, this book draws on a wide range of sources, from newspaper articles to poetry. It also includes stories and memories, published and unpublished, including some interviews or 'oral histories' that have been commissioned specifically for this book. Given the intensity with which the riots are remembered in Liverpool, it would be impossible to include as many 'oral histories' as we would have liked, and we have had to make choices, trying to include voices from as many sections of the communities as possible: people who rioted and those who did not; individuals and members of community organisations; activists, politicians and professionals; ordinary people and establishment figures, including key figures in the Anglican and Catholic churches, and former police officers. The people who told us their stories or provided other stories and images in the making of this book are introduced in Table 1.

Alongside these personal stories and images, we have brought together a range of previously published but sometimes hard-to-access secondary material including reports by government bodies and community groups, which together will provide a valuable sourcebook. These provide insights into the wider context in which the Liverpool riots took place, and the aftermath of these events – the reactions by officials and community leaders who tried to understand what had happened and why, and who looked for solutions to the problems they identified. These include enquiries into policing, racism, and the roles of churches and community organisations in inner cities. Most of these investigations addressed the events in Liverpool as part of a bigger picture, so, before looking at the detail of the riots in Liverpool, it is important to set these in context. The events in Liverpool were preceded by others in the St Pauls area of Bristol in 1980 and Brixton, South London, in April 1981, as well as Southall, West London, immediately beforehand. The key events on the streets were as shown in Table 2.

These events have been called a 'turning point in British politics' because they 'destroyed at a stroke the myth of police invincibility', and because they drew attention to wider social

Table 1: People whose stories are told in this book

Name	Background	Contribution
Paul Adams	A young man at the time, Paul had left Liverpool to work in Sheffield. He returned at the time of the riots.	Interview (August 2010)
Gideon Ben-Tovim	Gideon was Treasurer of the Community Relations Council at the time of the riots. He is an academic who helped produce evidence for the Community Relations Council (CRC) and the Liverpool Black Caucus, and became a leading city councillor. He is now Chair of the Liverpool NHS Primary Care Trust.	Interviews (October and November 2010)
Mike Boyle	A Liverpool-born black man, Mike grew up in Liverpool 8 and was a union shop steward in the 1970s. After being made redundant he completed a degree and taught history and sociology at the University of Liverpool until 2010.	Written statement (November 2010)
Wally Brown	Wally was born in Toxteth and went to school there until he was 16. He later served as the only black shop steward in a trade union for engineering workers. He became involved in voluntary youth work and education in Liverpool 8, setting up a Black Access course. Wally also contributed to and co-authored *The Gifford Inquiry* into the Liverpool riots. He served as Principal of Liverpool Community College.	Interview (October 2010)
Phillip Canter	Philip was a solicitor in Liverpool 8. He supported the anti-racist and anti-Nazi movements by representing those arrested on demonstrations. He has worked closely with the local black community and he represented black and white people arrested in the riots.	Interview (October 2010)

Name	Background	Contribution
David Copley	David was a Methodist minister at the Princes Avenue Methodist Centre between 1978 and 1986. He chaired the Methodist Centre at the time of the riots, and was involved in the CRC.	Interview (October 2010)
John Cornelius	A local writer and artist, John wrote and illustrated a book of short stories entitled *Liverpool 8*, which was first published in 1982.	Drawings of Liverpool 8
'David'	'David' (not his real name) is a Liverpool-born black man, who grew up in Toxteth. He was 16 years old at the time of the riots.	Interview (October 2010)
Claire Dove	Claire grew up in Liverpool 8 and witnessed the riots on the TV while living in the US. She is currently chief executive of a women's education provider, working with business and government on regeneration of Merseyside and the North West.	Interview (October 2010)
Jon Murphy	Jon joined Merseyside Police in 1976 as a constable. His first beat was in the part of Liverpool 8 that included the main riot areas. Jon became intimate with some of the people of the area before moving to Scotland Road. From January 1980 and during the riots in 1981 he joined the Force Support Group, later known as the Operational Support Division (OSD). He is currently the Chief Constable of Merseyside.	Interview (October 2010)
Derek Murray	Derek worked as an Assistant Warden at the Merseyside Caribbean Centre on Upper Parliament Street and had been involved in community politics around the city. He ran an antiques shop outside Liverpool 8 before becoming a documentary filmmaker.	Interview (September 2010)

Name	Background	Contribution
'Nick'	'Nick' (not his real name) is a Liverpool-born black man. He was 18 years old at the time of the riots. He'd moved from the Dingle to Liverpool 8 (off Granby Street).	Interview (January 2008)
Michael Simon	Michael was 13 at the time of the riots, a pupil at Shorefields, which he says was the 'biggest racially mixed school within Liverpool at the time'. He identifies as 'mixed race'. During the riots, he spent two days and nights on the streets. Later he was arrested at home and spent five days locked up, then served two and a half months in a Young Offenders' Centre before being released without charge.	Interview (August 2010)
Goff Tinsley	Goff taught photography in the late 1970s and was also a driving instructor in the 1980s working in Toxteth. He witnessed the burning of the Rialto on 4 July 1981, and later returned to take photographs of the aftermath.	Provided photographs

and economic tensions that could no longer be ignored.[3] This national summer of discontent, in which Liverpool featured so prominently, provoked a series of reactions by the British government, which formed the official response to the riots. An enquiry into the events in Brixton, headed by Lord Scarman, was extended when the disturbances spread to Liverpool and beyond. Other official inquiries into inner-city deprivation and inequality included the Gifford Report (1989), which looked specifically at Liverpool, and Lord Swann's Inquiry into the Education of Children from Ethnic Minorities (which reported in 1985), which was widened to address issues raised by the riots. The Liverpool riots have also been explored in a series of scholarly

Table 2: Events of 1981

Date (in 1981)	Location	Event
10–12 April	Brixton	Riots: 226 casualties; 196 arrests
3 July	Southall	Clashes between Asian youths and skinheads
3–6 July	Liverpool 8	Riots sparked by arrest of Leroy Alphonse Cooper. CS gas used in mainland Britain for first time
7–8 July	Moss Side, Manchester	Riots. Police station attacked
11–12 July	20 locations including Liverpool, Hull, Leeds, Leicester	Disturbances and riots
26–28 July	Liverpool 8	Riot following death of David Moore under police vehicle
11 August	Liverpool	Funeral of David Moore: conflict with police.
15 August	Liverpool	Anti-police march

articles, some of which are now difficult to find, but which have stood the test of time and warrant republication. These include, for example, an essay on the ways in which the national news media represented Liverpool 8 as the backdrop to the riots, and another on the ways in which the riots raised questions about policing. Extracts from these papers, reprinted here, provide wider context and critical distance on the disturbances of 1981 and also on the ways in which these were addressed at the time.

At the heart of this book, though, are the voices of people who experienced the riots and their aftermath, so it is appropriate that these people should have the last word. In the following extracts, a number of individuals look back on the riots and reflect on their legacy. The general points they raise here are examined in more detail in subsequent chapters, which focus upon particular kinds of memories and legacies. These include 'Nick', then an 18-year-old who lived off Granby Street:

I think what was scary about it was the police standing there with these batons, and then banging the batons on these shields, like as if it was a war. I suppose that's the way they had to try and intimidate people to get them off the streets. But, I think it did the opposite. I think people started saying, 'look that's a gang, and we're a gang' – it did the opposite. It completely did the opposite.

Jon Murphy, a senior police constable in Liverpool 8, described the view from the other side of the police lines and reflected on the racial dynamics of this.

The police stood behind shields and, and you could look back at it now and think what a futile exercise that was ... the police just stood behind shields, while people threw petrol bombs at them ...

I don't think it was a race riot [but] we had a lot of disaffected black youth, partly because the police were not sensitive in the way they dealt with it, they weren't trained to deal with it. It was something that was new to them.

Questions of race and community policing are never far from the surface in memories of the riots. The length of the chapter on policing in this book testifies to the strength of feelings on this subject. Introducing a theme that will be developed in this book, community activist and academic Gideon Ben-Tovim argues that while many people used the riots to raise their own agendas, the central issue for most people was policing:

We had one perspective that said it was all about criminal gangs and outside hooligans, and the other perspective that said it was all about unemployment. Both of those missed the point about the sharp reality of issues around police–community relations that was at the heart of it, even though other factors might have impinged.

The last word in this Introduction goes to 'David', then a 16-year-old resident of Liverpool 8, who conveys another theme running through many memories and narratives of the riots, and perhaps suggested in John Cornelius's drawing, 'All riot on the night' (Figure 0.1): a sense of unity and release. 'I'm trying to restrain the euphoria, even after all this time I can feel a rush.' He remembered:

> To see the power of people, a community united as one with one target. People actually standing together and drawing their line in the sand: 'That's it, we've had enough, this is payback'; to see the people actually succeed. People may call it anarchy, but this was a message from the people. They come together and fought. People still willing to take on the police despite their numbers, despite the hi-tech equipment the police had at the time, and they won! Can you imagine that, to see them running, to see officers actually getting up and running away?

Notes

1   John Cornelius, *Liverpool 8*, illustrated by the author (London: John Murray, 1982), pp. 119–21.
2   CARF (Campaign Against Racism and Fascism) Collective, 'The Riots', *Race and Class* 23.1/3, pp. 225–27.
3   CARF, 'The Riots', pp. 225–27.

1

What Happened:
Experiences and Memories

Memories of the Liverpool riots are everywhere: posted on the internet, included in memoirs and biographies, presented more formally in surveys and reports, and stored in photographs, taken at the time and carefully preserved. A selection of comments and memories, posted recently on the internet in forums on the riots, illustrate how these events live on in the city's collective memory and identity.

I was only ten when the riots occurred but I remember fainting in assembly that morning as my mum had to go and help my Granddad check on his electrical shop on Upper Parliament Street and I was scared she would not come back! The shop was later demolished due to fire damage on the adjoining buildings.[1]

I lived in Mulliner St and remember the kids pinching the shoes out of the shoe shop and running down our street with them. It was really funny because they were all left shoes off the display and they were trying to sell them.[2]

I was 11 years old when this was happening and it was very scary. I lived on St Saviour's Square on the Falkner housing estate [which] was like a rabbit warren and I always remember looking out from the upstairs bedroom window to see the street lights being taken out, leaving the place plunged into

darkness. Monday morning and it was like a war-zone. I had
to pick my way through all sorts of debris in order to get to
school, although we seemed to have an awful lot of McVitie's
Jaffa Cakes in the cupboard at that time too!!![3]

At the time of the riots I was living in a flat near Princes Park
Gates. I remember drinking in town and finding that the buses
that went along Princes Avenue had all been cancelled. It
was only a twenty-odd minute walk home anyway (but buses
were regulated and cheap in those days!) and I remember us
walking up the centre of the Boulevard and we were the only
people walking in that direction; there were loads of people
walking towards town to watch or join in. When we got home
we climbed out onto the roof and couldn't believe our eyes.
The Rialto was in flames, as was what looked like the entire
length of Lodge Lane. As for Smithdown Road, I was told that
gangs of scallies took advantage of the diversion occupying
the police elsewhere to break into Sefton General Hospital,
ransack all the tobacconists' shops on Smithdown Road (with
taxis kept waiting for them outside), and even the undertak-
er's at the top of the road a few doors from The Boundary was
ransacked. I was told that even the corpses had been tipped
out of the coffins.[4]

I was eleven when the Toxteth Riots took place. For me it was
an exciting time. At that time I was unaware of the reasons for
the riot but realised that there seemed to be a lot of baiting
going on from both sides.[5]

These internet postings are just the tip of an iceberg, which this
chapter investigates in more detail. It begins by quoting from a
series of oral histories, in which people who were involved in or
affected by the riots tell their stories. It then includes a section
drawing on internet postings and published documents, which
present eye-witness accounts of what happened in Liverpool in
July 1981.

Personal Stories

The oral histories conducted for this book illustrate the ways in which the riots were experienced and how they have been remembered by people who lived in Liverpool at the time. 'David', who was 16 at the time, describes how he reacted to news of unrest:

> I remember the night one of my sisters had come home and was talking about what had happened that day and the previous night. I recall her stating how we're not taking any of this shit and how this was going to stop. From the description she gave it was like someone had had a 'straightener' with a few police officers, not the first time I may add. That they had stood up to the police after another attempted arrest of another black youth and the community decided to say enough was enough. The police called for reinforcements and when they arrived they were stoned back out of the area. From that day onwards it just escalated into a full-scale riot.
>
> A family friend then told me that they were on their way home from town on a Saturday night and when they gave instructions to the driver as to where they wanted to go the taxi driver informed them that he was unable to 'go up that end of town love there was murder with the police'. They then decided to make their way up there and saw for themselves first-hand what was occurring.

'David' continues, describing the intensity of the riots as they ran into a second and third night:

> We'd heard about it and after the second night had gone off … me and my mates, who lived on Park Road and the other side of Windsor Street, [we] went up to see what was happening and what we saw was just mesmerising. There it was lines of them, hundreds of 'Thatcher's Bastards', standing in lines across the road behind Perspex riot shields. Initially there was

about a thousand people standing about on Kingsley Road, the opposite side of Kingsley Road, Myrtle Gardens and up as far as the top of Parliament Street. This was an awesome sight, a bit frightening, especially when they started beating upon their riot shields; the noise was a loud intermittent banging of shields.

Well, initially, hundreds of people had gathered and more and more people would come as it got darker. By night time you had to ask yourself were there this many people in the community? ... No, there were people there from all over the city [and] from all over the country. It seemed like anyone that had ever suffered at the hands of the police or the economic circumstances of a Thatcherite government [was there].

Others heard about the riots through the media. Claire Dove, who grew up in Liverpool 8, was overseas at the time:

I was living in the United States when the riots happened. It was quite amazing when I switched on the television to recognise people I knew from our area. When I eventually arrived home it was to major devastation, right down Parliament Street, buildings I had known since childhood were just gone. For my mother, who lived just round the corner from Parliament Street, it was traumatic and very frightening. One of my brothers was hurt quite seriously. He was trying to run home and got hit very badly on the head, and then they talked about the abuse of the police. So it was alarming to come home at that time, very alarming.

Michael Simon, a 13-year-old who lived off Granby Street, spent three days out on the streets during the riots, during which he 'couldn't get home'. He describes what happened and how he got involved:

It started off with two guys and one of them, a huge guy, 6ft 4, started to go round and started confronting the police on the beat, just going round punching them basically and this kind of escalated.

For me, it just seemed like this was the beginning of a war if you like because there was an option, the future for me was like you grow up, the police will arrest you whenever they want, they'll beat you up and you will have a criminal record if they say you do. It was just quite scary really, looking back on it now, but in my own mind, it was wholly justified, every single part of it.

The only thing I can make the analogy with is like in a war situation, where you see people doing things which you're just thinking 'fantastic', you realise it but you're actually inspired by these things, by what some people are doing and the solidarity, there was none of this leaving people alone. There were incidents where people were getting arrested and we'd surround the police van and pull them out ... but after that then the ... police were becoming more and more protective and the violence got more. The police were getting a lot more violent, a lot more equipped and were just basically ramming people, they were calling it 'dispersal' at the time, it was basically ramming people. I always remember this guy running because we were all running and he was hobbling and I thought he'd hurt his leg, it wasn't until later that you [realise he was shot in the leg]. But I remember we ran that way, because we were running to the fence, thinking they couldn't get past a concrete bollard, and this guy just went that way and, well, the Jeep just flattened him, went right over him. I think he died there and then, or died within about 10 minutes, and he was disabled. David Moore, a disabled guy, so apparently he couldn't get out [of] the way. That was a really, really violent night, that night.

People were saying, the Jeeps that they brought in [were] from Northern Ireland, they looked exactly the same, they could get over the estate which was where you ran to because it had graduations and hills but they could get over that.

I was a witness when David Moore got killed as well but I couldn't even go to court because I was on a curfew. I witnessed him getting killed, right in front of me.

On the Saturday, I always remember by 3.00pm there was a crowd of at least 2000 already waiting on Granby Street and I think the off licence door had been wrecked on Kingsley Road, Avis had already been wrecked, but this crowd was just going and going. It stopped from being kind of like tit for tat and hit and run and just started as a stand-off fight if you like. Occasionally the police would do a charge but even after the crowd swelled, and it was getting bigger, that stopped and when it came to the Sunday, they just literally downed shields and started running away. The CS gas was going as well – I remember seeing Paul Casey [not his real name] on the floor after he'd been shot, I didn't see him shot but seeing him on the floor.

I managed to get in about, must have been 5 o'clock Monday morning, I got up with sticky eyes with the CS gas and so we were just a crowd down the bottom, you're talking about a big crowd and then the next minute vans just come from everywhere and I wasn't running because it's my street, big mistake, it didn't matter to them, they started waylaying into everyone and [arresting them], started filling the vans up.

I was the only one [in the family] that got arrested. [The police] just burst into the house and arrested me. Got absolutely battered as well, got drove round for half an hour, got battered. I remember getting battered and it not hurting, I don't know whether that's an adrenalin rush, I thought they were going to kill us because as you're growing up you do hear incidents of people [dying]. They drove us round for about

half an hour, it was Welsh coppers as well. Took us to Cheapside, battered us again. I spent five days in Cheapside, which
at the time was [tiny] Victorian cells but it was like 25 in a
cell, so if you think about how many cells are in Cheapside, it
was 25 in a cell and some of us, they only had them Victorian
benches, the flat ones which were maybe about as big as that,
so 6 or 7 of you could sleep at the time, the rest just literally
had to stand up around the cell and that, didn't get a thing to
eat. Looking at it now, these were grown men and we were
kids! Not that you felt like that, I thought they were gonna
kill us, I thought we'd got off lightly anyway, I really did think
they were going to kill us in there.

Community leaders offer broader perspectives of the riots as
they unfolded. Wally Brown, a youth and community worker,
was called to a disturbance, which had taken place after a police
sweep, in which officers 'went round arresting people ... they
recognised probably from when the kids were stoning the vans':

> So, when I got there, it was the junction between Grove
> Street, Parliament Street, on the corner by the Caribbean
> Centre. There'd been some workmen doing some work, and
> there was a worker's cabin on wheels ... and they set that on
> fire, the kids. I remember saying, there were no police there
> then, just the kids all milling round. They'd set it on fire ...
> and started to set barricades up across the street. I said 'The
> police are going to come' ... I said 'You're going to get arrested
> ... you're all going to get in trouble'. But the police never came.

Wally Brown also remembers cars being stopped and taken off
people. They were turned over, set alight and used as barricades.
He recalls these being used as a 'block-off' between Grove Street
and the two ends of Parliament Street. He continues:

> Probably the worst part for me was watching innocent people
> getting cars taken off them, getting cars hijacked and people

just driving through, not realising what had gone on before the word got round ... and all of a sudden, they are in this situation ... and that for me was terrible. But eventually word got round ... 'don't go round there', the buses stopped running that way and people stopped going that way ... and the street was just occupied by the kids – a mixture of kids, black and white who lived there ...

David Copley, a Methodist minister, also experienced the riots at close hand.

As the pressure from the police was getting heavier and heavier towards black [people], particularly young boys, that sense of irritation and frustration grew into a real sense of anger and that was coming across very strongly to us. Part of their anger was that they were never allowed to feel at home. Whereas a very strong feeling amongst [the youth] was this was their territory, their home, and, as there would be in any kind of inner-city area, these are/were their streets and the police are invading them. I think there was a [feeling that] 'nobody's listened to our pain; we're not being listened to'.

Jon Murphy, then a police constable, gives another perspective on the same events. He recalls the role of the Operation Support Division:

We were the reserve that was brought out to try and relieve the pressure on the [police] who were behind the shields. Most of them were young lads, in a uniform, in shock. They were stood behind the riot shields. We would form up behind them at a point ... an instruction would be given and bear in mind we didn't have mobile phones then [and] the radios didn't work as well ... The line would part.

I remember one night in particular, and we were on Upper Parliament Street. There was a line across Upper Parliament

Street facing towards Smithdown Road and it would be at
the end of Grove Street Junction ... Grove Street, I think it's
Kingsley Road the other side ... So, the Wootton Centre is a
bit further up on the right, and it was the night the dairy was
broken into, and all of this stuff was coming over on fire, there
was a huge group had gathered at the Wootton Centre, which
was the headquarters, I think, for the Liverpool 8 Defence
Committee, and there was a huge group gathered there, and
the instruction we were given was to go and disperse that
group of people ...

The shield line split. We came out [with] the vehicles. There
were probably three or four other Land Rovers with us, and
a couple of personnel carriers. So, maybe twenty of us. I was
actually the acting Sergeant in the group, because my Sergeant
had been injured. We got out of the van, and we had batons,
and my wooden baton is about 18 inches long ... and then
we just sort of ran at these people, and I remember chasing
a particular guy across some wasteland, and I remember
distinctly because I've got all this heavy-duty kit on that wasn't
much use, but weighed me down, and I remember at the time
we used to call it rioters' gear, because they [the rioters] would
be in training shoes, track shoes and a vest, and a baseball
bat, or some other big stick of wood. That's exactly what this
guy had. It was a black guy as it happens, and I remember
chasing him across the wasteland, and he turned round and
he confronted me, and I looked around me and there was no
one anywhere near me, and I've got this little stick, and he's
got this big long stick, and I've just thought 'Oh dear, this is it'
... and my response was, 'I'll see you again', and I just retreated,
and went back ... and managed to get back to the vehicle.

Cars had their accelerator pedals tied down, the cars [were]
being set on fire, and driven straight at the police lines. I
remember javelins being thrown. I remember a school being

broken into, and javelins being taken out of the school sports cupboard and being thrown at the police cars. I remember one went straight through the hood of a personnel carrier, and hit the engine block. I remember axes being used and going through the sides of [vehicles]. We were in the back of the Land Rover and there was no light, and we would drive from behind the police line to try and relieve the pressure and then we could see nothing, we could just hear things hitting the side of the Land Rover and people trying to open the [vehicle]. It was pretty frightening stuff.

On one night there was something like 15 or 16 gas grenades thrown and probably 40 or 50 CS gas rounds. The clear view of the Chief Constable at the time was, if I don't do this, some of my officers will die ... and there's no doubt about it, he genuinely believed that, and having been there on the ground, I thought that was gonna happen anyway. I thought it's a miracle, frankly, that a police officer didn't die.

Goff Tinsley, a photographer, was working as a volunteer for Age Concern in Liverpool in 1981. On the evening of 4 July he was at a restaurant in Hope Street, celebrating his mother's 88th birthday, and on his way home came across the disturbances in the Toxteth area.

Hearing on the radio that things had quietened down on the Monday morning (although this was an uneasy quiet and the disturbances were not officially over for a week), I decided to take my camera to the affected area and make a personal record of the damage. This decision was prompted by a feeling of sadness as the area had suffered during the air raids in 1941, been rebuilt to a certain extent, and was now being destroyed again.

During the time I was walking about taking photographs I did not encounter any hostility either from the police, who were maintaining a presence in the area, or from the local inhabitants. I asked permission if I could take images of the people and talked to a few of them. One policeman asked what I was doing and I told him I just wanted to record the scene for posterity.

These personal stories were followed by more formal accounts of the riots, which came later in a number of forms including articles, memoirs, biographies and histories, written and published by individuals and in some cases on behalf of organisations. Prominent among these were church leaders, whose experiences and interventions played an important part during and after the riots.

The Churches in Liverpool

Church leaders and members, including those located in Liverpool 8 and others that expressed concern for people in the area, played an active part in seeking to understand the riots and to help those affected. The heads of the Catholic and Anglican Churches in Liverpool – Catholic Archbishop Monsignor Derek Worlock and the Rt Reverend David Sheppard, Anglican Bishop – acted together during and after the riots. They later described what they saw and did in a jointly authored book, *A Time for Healing* (1988), which included a chapter on 'Christian Partnership in a Hurt City'. Looking back, they reflect: 'The scars which Liverpool 8 bears to this time as a result of those nights of conflict are by no means restricted to burnt-out buildings'.[6] But their account has an optimistic subtext, speaking of cooperation in a time of crisis, and anticipating wider developments within faith communities, which addressed some of the problems of British inner cities (see the discussion of the *Faith in the City*, the report published by the Anglican Church, in Chapter 4 of this book).

From A Time for Healing, *Derek Worlock and David Sheppard,*
1988

On the third evening in Toxteth, the pair of us went out
together ... We decided to go to the offices of the Merseyside Community Relations Council to see if there was any
way in which we could help. Just as we arrived, a young
black lad ran in with a message from one of the leaders of
the black community. He and his colleagues inside the ring
could not make themselves heard. Could anyone get hold of
two megaphones for them? [The bishops then persuaded the
police to lend megaphones, which they passed on to community leaders.]

With the megaphones under our jackets we made our way
out of the police station, through the unobservant press
reporters and back to the perimeter ring of police. We talked
our way through the lines and headed for Upper Parliament
Street. We were stopped by a couple of black middle-aged
somewhat aggressive men who did not recognise us and told
us to get out. It turned out afterwards that they were visitors
from Manchester who had come over to join in any trouble
which might be going. We managed to press on until we were
in sight of the particular community leader who had sent the
request. We decided that it might not make life easier for him
if at that point he was seen with us. We gave the megaphones
to two small boys and asked them to take our valuable cargo
to the leader. There was something almost biblical about the
scene as they ran off on this precious errand. A few moments
later we heard his advice carrying across the waste ground
to the crowds gathered about him. 'Go home,' he called. 'Go
home. You will be better there. There is no need for you to
be out tonight.'

As the crowds slowly dispersed, we made our way to another
sector of the area where with one of the local clergy we

walked the streets for the next three hours. Several large fires were burning and we sat with one of the priests in his house as he waited to see if the fire would be brought under control before it reached his church. It was a vigil which for several weeks became for us a nightly patrol: trying to sustain local clergy and parishioners, seeking to calm things down just by being seen on the streets each night, and to win the confidence of both the local community and the police.[7]

The leaders and members of other churches also took an active interest in the riots and their aftermath. David Copley, a Methodist minister, felt harassed by the media, which put pressure on him simply to condemn the riots, when he had a more nuanced message to get across:

On the Monday morning I was door-stepped at home, well I couldn't get out the house, the press were standing outside our house as they were various other people's homes, and all they wanted was ' give us the name of the leader'! What? It was unbelievable really, their reaction.

Archbishop Derek Worlock was in town ... and he came to see me to see what was going on and he said he'd had exactly the same thing. The press had come to him saying, 'presumably you're totally against it as a Christian' and 'who would the leaders be?' and he wasn't quite sure how to react. [The reporter] wanted to know what we [who were a bit closer to the local people] felt and that's how they started to consult with us really. Well how do I react to that question? Are we supposed to condemn this or are we not?

All credit to him [Archbishop Derek Worlock] and then Bishop David Sheppard who came back at the end of the week. Their response to the media frenzy was always measured, thoughtful, informed and compassionate.

I think the big miscalculation was that they [the press] thought the churches would all say it was wicked. I think they got a big shock when they found that not only did all the local clergy, Fr Peter Morgan at St Bernard's RC, Fr Colin Oxenforth at St Margaret's CE Church and me, all far from saying it was wicked or evil were saying it was, though not quite the opposite, it was the young people were on the side of the angels if anything and we tended to exaggerate the thing of course, (a) because I was a lot younger and (b) because you had to do, you just had to.

So then when the media turned from us [and] to the church leaders and found the same thing being said in more measured tones of course, but it was actually the same message, and that was very good.

The media's approach to the riots was something that David Copley, 'as somebody who tries to work in the forgiving business', has found 'very difficult to forgive'. But journalists and press photographers, telling their own stories, sometimes present a more sympathetic picture, as the next case history illustrates.

Press Photographer[8]

In 1981 Tony Hall was a photographer with the Mercury Press Agency in Liverpool. He was called out to take photographs during the riots, and reflected afterwards that the significance of the events did not sink until later.

I was at home, near Wigan, when our night reporter phoned me to say 'trouble had kicked off in Toxteth' and they needed a photographer as soon as possible. I assumed it would all be over by the time I drove back into the city and suggested that they get one of our other photographers who lived in Bootle. How wrong could I have been? It was still going on weeks later.

Liverpool became the focus of worldwide media attention, and on the second night we were sent out on foot to get what we could, which is when everyone realised how serious the situation was, as petrol bombs were thrown at police lines and cars and buildings set on fire.

We had to take almost every picture without a flash, as you became a target if rioters saw the flash going off. I have never covered anything like it before or since.

We spent days and nights out on the streets as the situation escalated. It was our job and what we got paid for. Only when developing and printing the images later on did we finally realise the extent of the social breakdown that had occurred, and the shock of what was happening finally got through.

One of the earliest pictures, which I took on the second night of rioting, shows a thin line of police officers in normal uniform holding only plastic shields for protection as they attempted to regain the streets under a canopy of smoke from petrol bombs and burning buildings. It shows how ill-equipped the force was and how they were unprepared for such full-scale unrest.

When Lord Scarman was asked to prepare a report on the riots he requested that my image of the 'thin blue line' should be used on the cover. People have waited 25 years for change and the photographs may be fading, but my memories of those nights are not, and never will.

Community Organisation:
The Merseyside Community Relations Council

In its Annual Report for 1981, the Merseyside Community Relations Council (forerunner of the Merseyside Racial Equality Council) identified the riots as 'a watershed in the development of Race Relations on Merseyside', exposing problems and calling urgently for solutions.[9] 'No longer will it be possible, as so many have done over the past twenty years, to sweep real issues out of sight by claiming Liverpool as a mythical example of racial harmony.'

> At about 9.30 p.m. on Friday 3rd July 1981 a young black man on a motor bike was stopped by an unmarked Police vehicle at the junction of Granby and Selbourne Street. In response to a call by the Policeman for assistance in detaining the young man at least eight Police vehicles converged within a few minutes on the area. This heavy presence combined with a lack of any reason obvious to bystanders as to why the man was being detained, led to a crowd gathering, angry at what appeared to be yet another incident of harassment. A scuffle ensued during which the original youngster ran free but another local black, Leroy Cooper, was arrested for assaulting Police Officers. For the next four hours groups of young people wanting to express their anger at continual Police pressure, roamed the area and threw stones at any passing Police vehicle and about half a dozen had windscreens smashed. Anger was further accentuated both during the Friday night and during the day on Saturday as word spread of Leroy Cooper's arrest because it was well known that he and other members of the family had frequently been the subject of Police attention in the past and indeed a brother had only been acquitted on a charge in the Crown Court the day before. In fact the Cooper family had been the subject of specific representations by the CRC and others to Senior Police Officers on several occasions prior to this incident.

This incident which triggered the riots of Saturday and Sunday is mentioned in some detail, because it is important to remember that the disturbances originated from a deep-seated anger directed at the Police as a result of years of daily incidents. It is also not accidental that the triggering incident happened within the black community as they have been the butt of the racist prejudices and behaviour of at least some Police Officers.

Full-scale rioting erupted late on Saturday evening and there followed a night of fighting against the police, mainly in the area of what has come to be the battleground of the top end of Upper Parliament Street. Fighting continued until about 8.30 in the morning, a number of properties were burnt, but little or no looting took place that night.

The most ferocious battle developed on the Sunday night as what had started within the black community expanded with youth both black and white coming in from surrounding areas. About 10.30 p.m. the police lost effective control and their cordon which was slowly pushed back down Upper Parliament Street did no more than provide an enemy and a focus to the battle. As the rioters advanced, properties were fired that were seen as being commercial like the furniture warehouse in the old Rialto Building or as irrelevant to the community like the Racquets Club. No arson occurred in residential properties or community centres. When there was a fear that the fire in the Racquets Club might spread to the Princes Park Geriatric Hospital next door, local people were instrumental in that the elderly residents were safely evacuated and taken out of the area, mainly in taxis.

While the riot battle raged down Upper Parliament Street the police abdicated the Lodge Lane and Granby areas and looting took place, especially in Lodge Lane. Significantly, almost no black people were involved in this and there are many stories which suggest that people from outside the area came in to profit from the confusion. During the looting properties were set alight and by the end of the night it was Lodge Lane that looked more of a disaster area than any other section of the district.

At about 3.00 a.m. the police without warning began to use CS Gas and eventually attacked back up Upper Parliament Street until they regained control by about 4.00 a.m. CRC staff and many others within the community were soon aware that at least two individuals had been struck by CS Gas projectiles and been seriously injured. We expressed our concern in early statements to politicians such as Mr. Whitelaw and were further horrified when press investigations eventually discovered that the police had used projectiles intended for siege situations and carrying a maker's warning that they could be lethal if used directly against crowds. We were further astounded when the Chief Constable was appointed to head the enquiry into the actions himself and his colleagues regarding the use of CS Gas. We expressed the view to the Home Secretary and the Chairperson of the Police Committee that an independent enquiry should have been instituted.

On Monday 6th July an informal network of people within the community including several CRC Executive and staff members, after urging the police to avoid aggressive tactics and to keep outsiders away from the area, went out on the streets with loud-hailers to encourage the youth to keep off the streets and to maintain peace. This initiative succeeded and an uneasy calm returned to Liverpool 8 although trouble erupted on that [night] and following nights in other areas of Merseyside and in other cities.

In the Merseyside Community Relations Council report, specific events are set in the context of wider tensions, including endemic racism:

People within the Community, and agencies such as our own, have for years pointed to the constant day-to-day tensions generated by Police behaviour and to the social and economic deprivations suffered so acutely by the black community. Up to now there has been little willingness to accept or understand the reality of this experience and there has been a severe lack of political will behind attempts to confront the issues and work for a genuinely multi-racial community in which all people irrespective of race are treated with respect by institutions such as the Police and provided with equal opportunity in access to employment and services. The event of July involved some of the worst rioting seen on British streets in the past century and it has been our concern since then to help ensure that politicians both locally and nationally make a real attempt to understand the reasons that fuelled such ferocious anger and resentment. We can only prophesy that such 'riots' will erupt again unless there is first of all a radical change in the manner of policing so that black youngsters can very quickly feel a change in the way in which they are treated, and unless in the longer term the processes and assumptions of racism are reversed both in society generally and in the way in which our institutions treat black people.

Even without the riots the past twelve months have been an unusually active and significant period for the Community Relations Council. There have been two themes of particular importance. The first, a negative one has been a marked upsurge in racist attacks on individual black people and their property since last summer. More positively the Liverpool City Council agreed in principle at the end of last year to Equal Opportunity Policy and the creation of a Race Relations Liaison Committee which since February 1981 has been the focus for serious consideration of race issues within the Council.

In this way, the Merseyside Community Relations Council looked beyond the immediate experience of the riots towards broader issues, stressing the scale of problems but also looking forward to solutions. The following chapters examine these developments, in which memories of the riots have been turned to positive effect, focusing on a number of themes. Issues of race and ethnicity cut through each of these, so they are addressed throughout this book rather than in a single chapter.

Notes

1   http://www.bbc.co.uk/liverpool/content/articles/2006/06/28/toxteth_anniversary_feature.shtm

2   Anonymous, http://www.facebook.com/topic.php?uid=112912126093 &topic =13105

3   Anonymous, http://www.facebook.com/topic.php?uid=112912126093& topic =13105

4   http://www.bbc.co.uk/liverpool/content/articles/2006/06/28/toxteth_anniversary_feature.shtm

5   Anonymous,http://www.facebook.com/topic.php?uid= 1129 12126093 &topic =13105

6   Derek Worlock and David Sheppard, *A Time for Healing* (London: Hodder & Stoughton, 1988; Harmondsworth: Penguin, 1989), p. 165.

7   Worlock and Sheppard, *A Time for Healing*, p. 165.

8   'Twenty-five Years On – Toxteth Riots Remembered', *Liverpool Daily Post*, 5 July 2006, http://icliverpool.icnetwork.co.uk/0100news/0100regional news/tm_objectid=17333527%26method=full%26siteid=50061%26headline=twenty-five-years-on---toxteth-riots-remembered-name_page.html.

9   Merseyside Community Relations Council, *Senior Community Relations Officer's Report*, 11th Annual Report (17 September 1981).

2

Police And Community

well dere woz Toxteth
an dere woz Moss Side
an a lat a addah places
whe di police ad to hide
well dere woz Brixtan
an dere woz Chapeltoun
an a lat a adah place dat woz burnt to di groun
burnt to di groun
burnt to di groun[1]

In this extract from a poem called 'Mekkin Histri', Linton Kwesi Johnson remembers the riots as events in which black communities stood up against the police, and he illustrates the prominence of Liverpool in this national story. Policing is the single most important thread running through narratives and reflections of the riots in Liverpool, ranging from personal stories through local political commentaries – including the interventions of Councillor Margaret Simey – and high-level government enquiries and reports, notably that conducted by Lord Scarman. The Conservative government then in office in Westminster tried to shift the focus of debate towards socio-economic issues and market solutions, as discussed in Chapter 5, and though economic aid was not unwelcome and somewhat successful, it did not deflect locally from the primary focus on policing. As the local Member of Parliament acknowledged, relationships between police and communities lay at the heart of the unrest. Richard Crawshaw, the SDP (Social Democratic Party) MP who represented Toxteth, acknowledged the need for a restoration of 'trust and confidence between the police and the community', making the following statement in Parliament:

> I do not believe that unemployment was the cause of the trouble, nor is it correct to blame it on the housing in that area. The area of the rioting has many thousands of new houses. I believe that these events came about because, rightly or wrongly, there is a genuine belief not only in the black community but in the white community that in that area the enforcement of law and order is not even-handed.[2]

Other respected observers reinforced this point. Derek Worlock, the Catholic Archbishop, told *The Times* newspaper 'that there was evidence that, despite some efforts by community workers and by the police themselves, there had been long-term mistrust between the black community and the police'.[3] He added that, for many disenfranchised local people, the police were not only held accountable for their own actions; they were also regarded as the representatives of a society that had excluded 'the only representatives whom Liverpool black people would meet of the wider society, which had 'excluded [them] from its normal life and opportunities'.[4]

Some people felt that the riots of 1981 were the inevitable outcome of a history of police harassment, intimidation and brutality inflicted on the Liverpool 8 black community. The Chief Constable of Merseyside, Kenneth Oxford, fuelled this view. On one occasion he repeated damaging, hurtful and racist claims that had been printed in the BBC's *Listener Magazine* about Liverpool's so-called 'half-caste problem' (emphasis added):

Policemen in general and detectives in particular, are not racialist, despite what many Black groups believe. Like any individual who deals with a vast cross-section of society, they tend to recognise that good and evil exist, irrespective of colour or creed. Yet they are the first to define the problem of half-castes in Liverpool. *Many are the product of liaisons between Black seamen and white prostitutes in Liverpool 8, the red light district.* Naturally they grow up without any kind of recognisable home life. Worse still, after they have done the rounds of homes and institutions they gradually realise that they are nothing. The Negroes will not accept them as Blacks, and whites just assume they are coloureds. As a result, the half-caste community of Merseyside – or, more particularly, Liverpool – is well outside recognised society.[5]

On other occasions, the Chief Constable made some equally problematic assertions about criminal tendencies within Liverpool's black communities. In evidence to the Scarman Inquiry (discussed later in this chapter), he complained of 'natural proclivities towards violence' in Liverpool 8.[6] Stories and allegations of discriminatory and racist attitudes extend from Oxford, at the top of the police hierarchy, down through the ranks. This chapter investigates these and others like them, quoting from a range of oral histories and published documents, and sifting through the evidence to present as broad a picture as possible of these experiences and issues.

Personal Stories

The police are central to most people's accounts of the riots, as the stories and memories quoted throughout this book illustrate. Many remember intensely negative feelings towards the police. Michael Simon, though just thirteen at the time, already had a string of bad experiences:

You had instances, especially with my brother, I remember many times being beat up by the police, not even arrested sometimes, just beat up, I remember my mum being arrested for protecting my brother, going down on Granby Street and jumping on top of my brother so he wouldn't get battered, she got arrested as well and went to court and you had all of this, them getting falsely imprisoned for robbing – I remember one instance, my brother was accused of robbing lead off a roof, which was a flat roof, but apparently the judge said 'you must have stashed it there' and that's how he directed the trial.

So you're aware of these type of things that go on and so you grow up with a deep hatred of the police and the system as well and I can remember that was burning with everyone, that was probably instilled from my father but you know, it was definitely like from my own observations and from my own experience during that period. It was deep, deep hatred of the system if you like and the police were just at the forefront of that for me. You were getting picked on. ...

If they're going to pull you and just charge you for whatever they want, you just lose all respect for them. I remember one copper called Sergeant B and he would just do whatever he wanted, there was another one who eventually ended up corrupt called Bernard [not his real name], he used to just kick the shit out of people in the street, there was nothing you could do about it at all and if you did complain, you'd just be arrested and they'd just make a charge up.

So during that period, I specifically remember because they had plenty of incidents where – it wasn't just like an explosion, it was kind of like a build up – you had so many incidents of people just about having enough so rather than standing passively and shouting names at the police when they were arresting someone, there were a few incidents. I remember someone getting arrested on Granby Street, I remember that kind of turning into a bit of a flashpoint and that was maybe two weeks beforehand.

Distrust of the police was not only common among men and boys. Claire Dove, who grew up in Liverpool 8, explains:

> There had always been issues with the police and the racism that many of us faced in our communities so from stop and search to unprovoked violence was an everyday occurrence. Even women were abused, I remember a young woman severely beaten by the police outside a local youth centre. The riots were not just about the inequality that we faced but also the oppression and racism of the police. In fact during the riots, police were drafted in from around the country as they took the local police off the streets. Many remarked that these police treated people differently.

And others suggested that the police were not only hard on black and ethnic minorities, but on others too, including working-class people of all backgrounds. 'Nick', who was 18 and lived off Granby St, reflects:

> I also think it had a lot to do with the way the government were treating working-class people and ethnic minorities at that time. They felt they didn't have the same rights as other people. They felt they were being picked on. More people being arrested for no reason. The areas were being policed a lot stronger. ... I couldn't go nowhere without being stopped and searched, and eventually you started getting mad, like 'what have I done, mate?' you know, I'd never been in trouble.

Community Leaders and Public Figures

Community leaders corroborate many of the claims and complaints made in personal stories and memories. Gideon

Ben-Tovim, who was involved with the Community Relations Council, explains:

> The concern of all of us from the CRC point of view was problems with the police, with young people getting into trouble often in our view for no good reason, with the courts often colluding with the police as part of a whole system involving people getting prison sentences or criminal records for sometimes trivial offences. By the end of the 1970s there was clearly a lot of tension building up in terms of the relationship between the police and the community, young men in particular.

Phillip Canter, a solicitor in Liverpool 8, recalls 'a time in which there were very bad relations between the police and the general public and also between the police and some of the local solicitors, including us':

> Just to give an example of this, I was in close touch with the then Chairman of the Police Committee, Lady Simey, and she and I were working together in trying to make a dossier of cases ... We'd had quite a number of cases in which we had been acting for particularly black young people, who had been arrested and turned out to be wrongly arrested, and were acquitted on trial. I had a folder with many cases in this, and we were on the point actually of making this public, when the riots took place.

> Another example of the difficult relationships we had particularly with the police was that at one stage ... the local bobby on the beat was instructed to stand outside our office, clearly discouraging people from coming in. We protested strongly against that, and eventually it was taken away and he didn't stand there any more. But that's an example of the sort of relationship we had.

> We were clearly not very popular because we were acting for a lot of people who were being acquitted or various matters were coming out in court which the police didn't like.

> The attitudes of police officers [led to] a general feeling of tension. When we cross-examined them in court, there was [a feeling] that here's a firm of solicitors that was set up to help these black people who didn't need helping ... and that sort of thing.

It is also important to acknowledge that generalisations about the police were qualified by some, who felt that at least some police officers were seeking better relationships with members of Liverpool's black and minority ethnic communities, and reflecting critically on their own police work. David Copley (Methodist minister) acknowledges tensions but resists generalisations:

> Before, contacts with the police were very difficult. Margaret Simey, who was our local County Councillor and Chair of the Police Authority, was a good friend and was so frustrated by their attitude to people, not just black people but the rest of us, who were the vociferous people in the CRC and so on. There was that very strong feeling that Oxford was utterly contemptuous.

> The community bobby for Granby was a nice fellow and he was on one of our committees. He was good, very pleasant, very hale and hearty, but if he walked into any of the Youth Centre activities at night, he would empty the room! [He] was perceived by kids as being just the same as the rest. I think that the general attitude was, it was institutional racism of course, but in addition to institutional racism I think there were out and out racists who were police officers and they took it for granted that black people were, by the nature of their 'different racial origin', suspect. It was part of the whole warp and weft of the Force.

There were one or two fairly decent officers. Our community officer, to be fair to him, was quite liked by some of the more senior members of the community and they sort of trusted him and he was a bit of an intermediary between there and Hope Street Police Station and so on but I don't think as far as the kids were concerned that made any difference at all.

Remembering this period, former Police Constable Jon Murphy is variously critical and defensive of policing at the time, acknowledging that some forms of policing were provocative but also challenging some claims that have been made about tensions between police and communities. He begins by suggesting that tensions between police and communities may have been exaggerated, and that relations were 'reasonably harmonious' on his beat (Catharine St, Crown St and Myrtle St). But he goes on to say that 'power was from time to time used inappropriately' and to concede that 'police just weren't sensitive to racial issues':

> There was no extraordinary level of tension between the police and the community at the time I was walking the beat there … and at the point when the riots broke out, it was a surprise to me.

> There were sus laws. I don't think the sus laws were used in this city anything like as much as they were for example, in London. Those powers were used to stop lots of people, not just young black people. But there was clearly an issue with young black people [who] were disproportionately affected by poverty, disproportionately involved in crime, as a consequence of being poor, and for no other reason, and that from time to time brought them into confrontation with the police.

> The 'suspected person loitering' was a power that existed to allow police officers to stop people if they thought they were

behaving suspiciously. Ask them to account for their behaviour. Probably search them, and what that power did was [to give] the officers an ability to arrest people for loitering before they'd actually committed an offence, because it was a preventative power that had existed for a hundred years ... and in some areas, I think that clearly that power was from time to time used inappropriately. If you saw somebody loitering down a back alley for example, where some houses had been burgled over a period of time, then that would be an appropriate use of the power perhaps. But in some instances, in some places, that power was abused.

There's no doubt about it, the police just weren't sensitive to racial issues in the way they are today. You know, inclusivity, diversity were not words that were in the police lexicon, and it was, I guess, a recipe for what happened.

But neither the Methodist minister's sense that there were 'one or two fairly decent officers', nor the police officer's measured account of policing at the time, contradicts the overwhelming sense that there were deep and growing problems with policing, and that these more than anything else lay behind the riots. Minister David Copley continued:

The burnings of buildings were always ... by-products of the main issue which was of course their [the community's] relationship with the police. I remember somebody saying (who'd come back into the CRC offices) how they felt that they'd [the community] turned to that [burning building] almost out of frustration. ... The police were building up their resources, coming along with the rubber bullets and all that sort of stuff and they were going to really show people. But it was extraordinary how people weren't out of control.

Gideon Ben-Tovim puts this in context, referring to research he and University of Liverpool colleagues had conducted in the decade preceding the riots, and to evidence they submitted to a 1972 Parliamentary Select Committee on Police/Immigrant Relations:

> Some of the concerns were about harassment and excessive police violence towards black people: I remember somebody graphically saying that, 'you don't mind if you've been caught for something you've done and being put in the back of a police van, but you do mind being beaten up at the same time.' There were also trumped up charges, often trivial cases, and many involving police-defined offences such as resisting arrest or threatening behaviour, which could mean anything. There were also widespread allegations of drug planting ('agriculture') by the police. During this period of the 1970s there were two cases that became *causes célèbres* of people who were found to be not guilty and were therefore clearly planted with drugs. One was a man who worked for the Merseyside Community Relations Council, and actually trained the police basketball team and yet was accused of carrying drugs. He was a man of enormously upright character and found not guilty. In another case a well known local musician was also said to be carrying drugs and again was found not guilty. So those were two well known local people who were able to summon a lot of support, character witnesses and so forth.

> But not everybody had that sort of backing or profile. There were many cases of other people who, with less access to supportive resources, ended up in the criminal justice system with a sentence for trivial or unreal offences. This was part of the feeling of bitterness: people felt they were being picked on, abused, dealt with unfairly and there was a lot of evidence to say this was a systematic pattern.

> There was evidence that 'stop and search' powers were being abused, so that a disproportionate group of people were being charged under that sort of legislation. There was also a Task

Force who were particularly notorious for the sort of violence and racism of their attitudes and behaviour.

This was a key concern of the Community Relations Council at the time, this pattern of young people getting into trouble with the police, ending up with criminal sentences, some of them going to prison. So various schemes were introduced including 'Help on Arrest', to give guidance if arrested.

Individuals' reflections on the problems with policing in the 1970s and 1980s can be set alongside more systematic commentaries and evidence on the subject, gathered and produced by a series of organisations and inquiries, both local and national. The most significant of these are introduced with extracts in the following sections.

Critics of the Police:
The Liverpool 8 Defence Committee

Criticism of Merseyside Police focused on Chief Constable Kenneth Oxford, who had dismissed the rioters as 'a crowd of black hooligans intent on making life unbearable and indulging in criminal activities'.[7] Among Oxford's most vocal critics was the Liverpool 8 Defence Committee, which issued the following statement on 25 July 1981, entitled 'Why Oxford Must Go'.[8]

> The call for the dismissal of the Chief Constable of Merseyside, Kenneth Gordon Oxford, has been made by the Liverpool 8 Defence Committee, the Liverpool Black Organisation and the Liverpool Trades Council, all of whom remain firmly convinced that he is the prime obstacle in the way of any constructive dialogue between the police and the community. Our specific reasons are as follows:
>
> The responsibility for the fair and proper policing of any community lies with the Chief Constable. Oxford's own

racism, combined with his belief that tough and repressive policing methods are the best way of keeping order, have resulted in excessive police harassment, especially of black people, which stretches back many years. Oxford must take the ultimate responsibility for this.

Oxford's own racism is an established fact. He is well-known for making derogatory and racist remarks about the Liverpool 8 community. Despite the fact that it has been pointed out to him time and time again that the term 'half-caste' is racist and insulting, he continues to use it in public and has even defended the use of the word. Oxford's own racism allows his officers to give expression to their racism and to indulge in the harassment of the black community. If the Chief Constable is a known racist, how can he be capable of stamping out racism in his own police force? ... Oxford has shown himself to be incompetent as well as racist.

The Liverpool 8 Defence Committee followed through its complaints against the police by working with the Charles Wootton Centre to organise an anti-police march, which was also supported by the Liverpool Labour Party and Liverpool Trades Council.[9] This articulated dissatisfaction with policing that was expressed through other channels too, including the Liverpool media. June Henfrey wrote the following in the *Liverpool Daily Post* on 6 July 1981:

The people of Toxteth have long been dissatisfied with the type of policing they get. Some months ago a young white woman told me that she thought people in Liverpool 8 should be paid danger money for living there, not because of crime but because of the level of police activity. At least no one so far has suggested that the youngsters of Toxteth should be sent home. They are at home, and bitter though it may be not to find the promised land in a strange country, it is infinitely more so to be dispossessed in one's own.

Holding Police to Account: Margaret Simey

The most immediate local intervention on the subject of police and community came from Councillor Margaret Simey, Chairman of the Merseyside Police Committee. Simey was a respected local figure who invested heavily in working to improve relationships between communities and police, a project that involved robust criticism of the latter. Interviewed by Radio Merseyside in the heat of the moment, while rioting was taking place, she suggested that conditions in Toxteth were so bad that people there 'ought to riot' and that she would regard them as 'apathetic if they didn't riot'. Simey was widely criticised for these remarks, and she responded to this in a statement, issued on 30 July 1981.[10]

> Policing by consent has become policing by confrontation. It is to repairing this situation that we must urgently turn our attention.
>
> Toxteth has reached a position where, whatever the rights and wrongs, police are now against people and people are now against police. That will not do. My words were used because of a sense of total exasperation, almost despair, at the fact that those to whom local people should be able to turn to have matters such as these properly examined, are left totally powerless by the system which has been forced upon us. We are Councillors: we stand for election: we want to represent the people: we want their grievances examined.

Simey's relationship with the police, her insights into the problems in the culture of policing, are illustrated in her diary entries on an address she delivered to the local Police Federation on 12 November 1981, at the organisation's AGM.[11] Simey called for a 'new partnership between police and public, through the agency of the Police Authority', and sought to dispel perceptions that the organisation she headed was 'anti-police'. Her diary entry for 13 November 1981 vividly illustrates the culture of policing that she sought to confront:

> Picture a room with a low ceiling. Crammed with beery bulky men ... A jam-packed little platform: policemen are all so hefty! And in the middle of it, me, the victim, cooked up as an Aunt Sally for their fun and entertainment.

> [After her speech:] Up then gets this crude Scotsman, Jardine, and rants and roars in true Hitler style. I was sickened and appalled. He urged them into battle against the 'louts' of Toxteth. He went for the Bishop and the Archbishop (who are Bishop Tutu types) and me and the Police Committee, ranting and roaring in the best Hitler style. The audience loved it, shouted and cheered and gave him a standing ovation. I think they were half drunk ...

> But how hideously frightening, that that low lot of illiterates should be sent out on the streets of Granby to chivvy our young people.[12]

Simey did not merely criticise, though; she also proposed solutions that might improve relationships between communities and the police, and as Chair of the Police Committee she got involved in delivering those solutions through the principle of accountable 'partnership policing'. This, she explained, 'must be a living reality so that policing is based on mutual support, mutual understanding, mutual confidence'. She called specifically for a 'far freer exchange of information and ideas' between police and others, and for a fully accountable police authority.[13]

Simey followed through the agenda raised by the riots, both publicly and privately. Her commitment extended to private efforts to help individuals who were affected by these broader issues. For example, she submitted written evidence to support the defence of a young man who faced and was acquitted of various charges in April 1989.

> Regrettably ... there is and has been for many years, a clear feeling amongst the black inhabitants of Granby that if they go into town, they are liable to be stopped as if not allowed to be there, and 'turned back' by the police and told to go back 'where they belong'. Young blacks driving nice cars outside Granby are liable to be stopped and inquiries made as to their right of ownership.[14]

The broader agenda regarding policing, raised by the riots, also extended to police tactics. Police authorities, anxious that the riots had caught them unprepared, reacted by seeking greater powers, including access to what Simey dismissed as paramilitary tactics. Finally, Margaret Simey helped pave the way for the national enquiry that investigated the causes of the riots, particularly in the context of policing. Conducting an immediate consultation with the communities affected by the riots, and establishing a network of community liaison forums, she contributed preparatory work that fed into the Scarman Enquiry and the proposals it ultimately put forward.

National Responses: The Scarman Enquiry and Report

Debate following the disturbances in Brixton in April 1981, concentrated on the problems faced by inner cities, and raised questions about the policing of black and minority ethnic communities. These concerns were expressed in the agenda for the first major enquiry into the disturbances, the Scarman Enquiry.

Following riots in Brixton on 10–12 April 1981, in which petrol bombs were thrown for the first time in mainland Britain, Home Secretary William Whitelaw visited Brixton and on 14 April he appointed Lord Scarman to hold a 'local inquiry'. Its terms of reference were 'to inquire urgently into the serious disorder in Brixton on 10–12 April 1981 and to report, with the power to make recommendations'. The Inquiry was run by Lord Scarman, supported by staff from the Home Office and legal counsel. Evidence was heard from representatives of police, local government, community organisations and the Commission for Racial Equality. The Scarman Enquiry began preliminary hearings on 14 May, but following the riots in Liverpool, its terms of reference were widened to address the disturbances nationally.[15] The Scarman Report was published on 25 November 1981. Scarman found that 'complex political, social and economic factors' had created a 'disposition towards violent protest'. He determined the disorders were not planned but a spontaneous outburst of built-up resentment sparked by particular incidents. He found loss of confidence and mistrust in the police and their methods of policing. Liaison arrangements between police, community and local authority had already collapsed before the disturbances. He recommended concerted efforts to recruit more members of ethnic minorities into the police force, and changes in training and law enforcement. 'Institutional racism' did not exist, he said, pointing instead to 'racial disadvantage' and 'racial discrimination'. His warning was stark: 'Urgent action' was needed to prevent racial disadvantage becoming an 'endemic, ineradicable disease threatening the very survival of our society'. Positive discrimination to tackle racial disadvantage was 'a price worth paying'.[16]

Scarman received written evidence from organisations and individuals in Liverpool, and visited the city on 16 October 1981 – towards the end of his enquiry, which reported the next month – at the invitation of the Merseyside Police Committee, chaired by Councillor Simey.[17] Scarman explains:

In the discussion which ensued, reference was made to a number of the Working Party's conclusions: the theme of the discussion was how a relationship of mutual trust between the police and all elements of the community might be established. Improved training, consultation with local communities, a more sensitive approach by the police, the status of community liaison officers, policing methods, and lack of confidence in the police complaints procedure were among the issues discussed. Members of the Committee also referred to the concern they felt about the issues of police accountability, the operational independence of the Chief Constable and the role of the Police Authority; and about the serious financial burden which the present arrangements for riot compensation (which were based on the Riot (Damages) Act 1886) threatened to impose on the Authority.

Following a tour of Toxteth during which he briefly visited the local police station, Lord Scarman went to the Headquarters of the Merseyside Police where he met the Chief Constable, Mr Kenneth Oxford, senior officers, and representatives of the Merseyside branches of the Police Superintendents' Association and the Police Federation. Among the issues discussed were the impact of the disorders on the force, including its younger officers, the law on disorder, police training and the police complaints system.

Finally, Lord Scarman visited the Charles Wootton Centre, in Upper Parliament Street, Liverpool 8, where he met members of the Liverpool 8 Defence Committee. The Defence Committee Members emphasised the status of the well-established black members of the Liverpool 8 community as black Britons, not immigrants. In their view, police harassment over a long period, not unemployment, was the main cause of the disorders. The Committee cited various examples of alleged harassment, criticised the Chief Constable's report to his Police Committee on the disorders, and said that the enforced resignation of the Chief Constable was essential if police/community relations in Liverpool 8 were to be restored. They accepted the need for law and order to be preserved and for an effective police force: they objected, however, to police action during the riots, particularly in the use of CS gas, and to the heavy and abrasive way in which Liverpool 8 was policed. If this did not alter, the community as a whole; it was said, would oppose it. A change in the attitude of police officers was desirable, along with improvements in police training and a move towards community policing. Finally, the members of the Committee referred to a recent picket they had conducted of a Crown Court at which a youth arrested during the disorders was to be tried, and asked Lord Scarman about the law on contempt of court. Lord Scarman explained that simply standing outside court was not a contempt, although it might raise other questions such as obstruction of the highway. If leaflets were handed out to potential jurors or placards were displayed in such a way as to influence them, however, contempt would arise. He advised the Committee to avoid the possibility of laying itself open to contempt proceedings in future.

In the overview and conclusions to his report, Scarman acknowledged differences between Brixton, his prime focus, and other areas affected by riots, including Toxteth and Moss Side, but he also found that

> many of the features of deprivation and decay which characterise Brixton are there repeated. In Toxteth, for example, the number of unemployed registered at the Leece Street Employment Office fluctuated from 1976 to 1980 between 17,000 and 18,000, but in the twelve months from June 1980 to June 1981 the number had risen by 3,000 to over 21,000. Unemployment again appears particularly to have

affected young people, and within that group, young black people. Street crime is relatively high: in 1980, of the 995 recorded offences of robbery committed within the Mersey-side area, over 20% were committed in one of the two police divisions which cover the Toxteth area. According to the Chief Constable of Merseyside, the area has historically been one which is difficult to police. Relations between the police and the black community in Toxteth, as was made plain to me when I visited Liverpool, are in a state of crisis. While many of the older people look to the police to protect them and wish for an increased police presence on the street, the young are alienated and bitterly hostile. Significantly, the beginning of the disorders in Toxteth on 3–6 July 1981, namely the arrest by a police traffic patrol of a youth who had been riding a motorcycle, invites comparison with the beginning of the disorders in Brixton. In each case a minor incident set off a great riot. The elements of a deprived area, unemployment, and hostility between a high proportion of the youth of the local community and the police seem well established.[18]

Scarman concluded that the disorders in Brixton originated spontaneously and 'quickly became a riot, the common purpose of the crowds being to attack the police.'[19] Though the riots attracted outsiders including white people, who 'helped to make and distribute petrol bombs', the riots were neverthe-less indicative of broader social tensions, particularly tensions between black people and the police.

> And there can be no doubt that the rioters, both the young blacks whose spontaneous reaction against the police started it off and the supporters whom they attracted from Brixton and elsewhere, found a ferocious delight in arson, criminal damage to property, and in violent attacks upon the police, the fire brigade, and the ambulance service. Their ferocity, which made no distinction between the police and the rescue

services, is, perhaps, the most frightening aspect of a terri-
fying week-end.[20]

(It is also true that in Liverpool, the fire brigade were allowed
through on occasions and a 'ceasefire' was called to allow for the
evacuation of an old people's home.)

Scarman drew broader conclusions, related to Brixton but
also to other parts of the country:

(1) The disorders were communal disturbances arising from
a complex political, social and economic situation, which is
not special to Brixton.

(2) There was a strong racial element in the disorders; but
they were not a race riot.

(3) The disturbances on Friday and Saturday arose from
police action common enough on the streets of Brixton, but
the tension was such that each incident triggered off serious
disorder.

(4) Once begun, the disorders on the Friday and the Saturday
soon developed into a riot. The common purpose of the
two riots was to attack the police. But the riots were neither
premeditated nor planned. Each was the spontaneous
reaction of angry young men, most of whom were black,
against what they saw as a hostile police force.

(5) On Saturday, however, outsiders did participate in the
rioting. They were attracted into the action by the publicity
given to Friday's events. These people (some of whom were
clearly identified as whites) played a significant part in inten-
sifying the disorder by making and distributing petrol bombs,
which were used for the first time on the Saturday.

(6) The Sunday riots were sporadic and spontaneous in
character, stimulated almost certainly by the elation felt by
many youngsters at their success, as they saw it, in defying
the police with such dramatic results on the Saturday. No
doubt some people were also attracted to participate in the

disorders by the publicity which the media had given the events of Friday and Saturday.

(7) The riots were essentially an outburst of anger and resentment by young black people against the police.[21]

The Liverpool 8 Enquiry

In addition to the public enquiries and reports described, there were initially two main practical responses to the crisis in policing which the riots had exposed. One involved the promotion of community policing, in an attempt to re-establish policing by consent, and to reintegrate police into communities. This was not helped by the second measure, which involved reinforcing police reserves and resources, to better prepare them for any future disturbances. Toxteth was the most heavily policed area in Liverpool by early 1982.[22] The police frequently deployed armoured cars, riots vans and the new 'hard-line' Operational Support Division.[23] These initial attempts to reform policing were to come under scrutiny later in the 1980s, when Liverpool City Council commissioned a broader enquiry into race relations in the city. Heading the inquiry, Lord Gifford QC quickly came to the conclusion that not enough had changed in Liverpool since the riots, particularly in relation to policing. On 30 November 1988, after just nine days of hearings, Gifford's team – which included Wally Brown and Ruth Bundy – issued a statement expressing 'its shock at the prevalence in Liverpool of racial attitudes, abuse and violence', forcing the city to face up to the fact it had a 'uniquely horrific' problem. This established a new impetus to change, 'to ensure that racial prejudices can be broken down to the benefit of the whole community', to restore confidence in institutions including the police.[24] From his inquiry conducted in 1988, Lord Gifford concluded that there was still 'racism in the police' in Liverpool.[25]

The police interact upon race relations in Liverpool in a number of ways. On the one hand, the police have the capacity to play a major role in the promotion of good race relations in the city. It is to the police that the Black community should be able to turn when the racism committed against them takes the form of criminal assault, threats or damage. Their fineness in handling racist crimes could have a major effect in preventing their spread. Secondly, the police have the obligation to investigate and deal with those crimes, such as the selling of hard drugs, which have become rife in the community. If they perform their function professionally and effectively they will deserve the respect of the community. On the other hand, if the police themselves are infected by the very racism which they ought to be combatting, the consequences will be disastrous. More than any other public authority, the consequences of racial prejudice among police officers are immediate and traumatic, both to the individual and to the wider community. Unlike other authorities, the police can take away your liberty, their evidence can lead you into prison. A prison sentence, besides being a most ugly experience, will make it impossible for you to obtain many jobs. It is not therefore surprising that the dereliction of duty by police officers brings a most immediate and angry reaction from law-abiding citizens.

The 'bleak overall picture of racism in Liverpool found by Lord Gifford was illustrated through a personal experience, recounted to the inquiry hearings by a former community police officer and serving police officer, in his evidence on oath to the Liverpool Crown Court in 1988. The transcript of the hearing includes the following questions and answers during his evidence.

Q. Have you heard any police officers racially abuse any people while you have been present?
A. Yes.

Q. What sort of things were said?

A. Bad things referring to their colour. Different remarks about niggers and things like that.

Q. That was done in your hearing and presence, was it?

A. Yeah.

Q. Was that done by just one officer or more than one officer?

A. It's pretty rife. I mean policemen are no different from anyone else. You've got to be pretty naive if you think they are not colour prejudiced, some of them ... you get some good, some bad, some fair.

Q. Have you ever received any problems yourself while you were in the police force?

A. Me personally? Yeah.

Q. Why was that?

A. My wife's of mixed race; I was very friendly with the Black people in the area. I considered that I had done a very good job. I built up a trust which was frowned on by policemen, in that I was a traitor to them, or something like that and they got a hard time. I had obscenities wrote on my uniform and my locker. These things were reported.

Q. What sort of things did you have written on your uniform, on your locker?

A. On my helmet I had 'Yankee nigger lover'. That refers to me spending some time in America. On my locker 'don't speak to him, he's married a nigger'.

If this is the experience of a White serving police officer, it is not surprising that we have heard ... case after case of overt racist behaviour from police officers towards Black people.[26]

Gifford concluded that there was 'a crisis in Liverpool':

The Inquiry repeats the conclusion which was contained in the declaration of principles, that the situation with regard to racial discrimination in Liverpool is uniquely horrific. This Chapter, and the detailed examination which follows of each area of our terms of reference, sets out why we reached that conclusion. Racism in any form is horrific, because it represents an affront to the dignity of the human person, and the blighting of opportunities for happiness and fulfilment for reasons which are irrational and wholly unfair. There are many forms of racism in Britain in all the areas where Black people live; but drawing on our experience of many of those areas, we summarise the reasons why we find the situation in Liverpool to be unique:

- Because Black people in Liverpool have been denied access to jobs, even low paid jobs, more systematically and comprehensively than in any other major city of Black settlement.
- Because there has been a unique conjunction in Liverpool of both exceptionally high unemployment and patterns of racial discrimination.
- Because nowhere else in Britain are Black people so exposed to threats, taunts, abuse and violence if they go outside a confined area of the city; nowhere else is there such a devastating lack of mobility.
- Because expressions of outright racial hostility and contempt are used in Liverpool to an extent that would no longer be acceptable in other parts of the country.
- Because all this is happening in spite of the much longer settlement and greater integration of the Liverpool Black community.
- Because the Liverpool City Council, unlike most other inner city local authorities, has failed to develop lasting policies to promote equal opportunities in its own workforce and in the services which it provides.

For these six reasons we say that there is a crisis in Liverpool which must be faced, and tackled with goodwill and resources. If it is neglected, the consequences for the whole city are grave. There are many precedents, especially in the United States, of the price to be paid – in crime, drug abuse, dereliction and disorder – if the grievances of a racial minority are not redressed.[27]

What Has Changed Since 1981?

Since 1981, some areas of British policing have been reformed, while the interrogation of policing started by Scarman has been taken further. Scarman, looking back on his report relatively shortly after its submission, wrote an 'epilogue' reflecting on its potential impact:[28]

> [W]hat has happened to the Report and its recommendations? Have they been remaindered to a footnote in the history books? Have they made any impact? Has society reacted? Are things better, or worse, as a result of the Report? Or have we moved on our way to whatever may be our journey's end, uninfluenced by it?

> The story of the disorders themselves has proved to be itself a therapy. Although the Inquiry and Report are criticised by some for not inquiring in depth into specific incidents of alleged police misconduct, the story has been accepted as a faithful account of the course of events. The conclusion that the disorders were 'communal disturbances arising from a complex political, social and economic situation ... not special to Brixton' and that they were 'an outburst of anger and resentment by young black people against the police' is now beyond challenge and has become one of the unspoken assumptions upon which social and police reforms are discussed and promoted.

> *Policing:* When one turns to the finding that neither the police nor the local bodies can escape responsibility for the breakdown of relationships between the police and the community, a similar observation may be made. The police

have learnt the lesson: and their efforts to mend fences – particularly in Lambeth and Liverpool – are notably significant. The police are trying to recruit members of the ethnic minorities: they are already tackling the problems of training, supervision, and monitoring so as to eliminate, or at the very least to diminish, racial prejudice within the force; and the philosophy of the Home Beat Officer has been accepted and is being put into practice. A sad omission, however, is the lack of will to include in the Discipline Code a specific offence of racially prejudiced conduct.

The Report has helped to bring to public attention the vexed and controversial questions of police consultation and accountability. The need for consultation at local level is now fully accepted. The controversy over accountability is not yet solved. On neither question has the Report been ignored. Its recommendation for a statutory solution has been accepted, though opinions differ as to the nature of the solution. But two vitally important recommendations relating to the police are, I fear, very much more doubtful of implementation, namely:

- lay police station visitors; and
- reform of the police complaints procedure.

Both go to the root of the problem of public confidence in policing methods, attitudes, and conduct. One can only hope that there will be legislation on these two matters as well as on consultation and accountability when the new Parliament assembles.

Law reform: The Report has had, I believe, a negative success. It has killed stone dead the proposal for a new Riot Act. It has persuaded the authorities that there is no need to amend the law in order to impose a 'selective' ban on processions and street demonstrations. Panic legislation against the emergence of further disorder has been avoided. On the positive side, it will be necessary to maintain pressure for the implementation by statute of the police reforms I have mentioned and to ensure that any new statutory 'stop and search' power is subject to effective safeguards.

Social policy: There are still no signs of 'an effective co-ordinated approach to tackling inner city problems'. But government at all levels has reacted favourably, and in some respects strongly, to three particular needs exposed by the Report: housing; education; and employment. It is not possible even to hazard a guess as to the extent to which Parliament or government will be prepared to develop the Report's recommendation for positive discrimination in these areas. But, as the Report indicates, a start is possible on the basis of sections 35 to 38 of the Race Relations Act 1976. The principle is already in our law.

Conclusion: The Report has not been shelved. It is having a continuing influence on all concerned with community-police relations. Much remains to be done: but much has already been done. We are now, as a society, aware of the racial disadvantage under which many of the ethnic minorities labour, of their frustrations, and of the risk of alienation. We know that we are a multi-racial society and we are beginning to tackle the problems. Even if the Report had achieved no more than an awakening, it would have served a useful purpose. But it has, in truth, done much more, as is evident from the distinguished contributions to which these few words of mine are an epilogue.

Some of Scarman's recommendations have since been implemented. The Police and Criminal Evidence Act (1984), setting out the way police officers were to carry out their duties, provided specific codes of practice and established the rights of people detained by the police for a suspected crime or offence.

And, where Scarman did not go far enough, others have done so in subsequent years, particularly with respect to institutional racism. Scarman later acknowledged that he could have been 'more outspoken about the necessity of affirmative action to overcome racial disadvantage',[29] so it has fallen to others to be more outspoken, and to directly face up to racism in British policing. Official acknowledgement of this had to wait until an inquiry into the police investigation of the racially motivated murder of black teenager Stephen Lawrence in 1993. Leading the Inquiry, Sir William Macpherson concluded that the police had been incompetent but that they had also been guilty of 'institutionalised racism'. This can be understood as '[the] collective failure of an organisation to provide an appropriate and professional service to people because of their colour, culture, or ethnic origin. It can be seen or detected in processes, attitudes and behaviour which amount to discrimination through unwitting prejudice, ignorance, thoughtlessness and racist stereotyping which disadvantage minority ethnic people.'[30] Specifically, the Inquiry found that

> [u]nwitting racism can arise because of lack of understanding, ignorance or mistaken beliefs. It can arise from well intentioned but patronising words or actions. It can arise from unfamiliarity with the behaviour or cultural traditions of people or families from minority ethnic communities. It can arise from racist stereotyping of black people as potential criminals or troublemakers. Often this arises out of uncritical self-understanding born out of an inflexible police ethos of the 'traditional' way of doing things. Furthermore such attitudes can thrive in a tightly knit community, so that there can be a collective failure to detect and to outlaw this breed of racism. The police canteen can too easily be its breeding ground.[31]

This recognition of institutional racism finally completed a process of interrogating racism in British society, which had its origins before 1981, but which was brought into the limelight and onto the national political agenda through the riots that took place that year.

But what do people in Liverpool 8 feel about the question of how policing has changed since 1981? Most acknowledge that policing has changed, generally if not always for the better, since 1981. Wally Brown is less directly involved in these issues than he used to be, but he suspects that 'police relations in general have got better, in terms of the big picture'. Gideon Ben-Tovim acknowledges that some changes and reforms have taken place since the riots:

> In the immediate aftermath there was a strong national as well as local reform movement around policing, triggered by the Scarman Report, so I think on reflection one of the legacies was a gradual improvement in police–community relations. That took quite a while to get there, and there was a serious flare-up of police–community tension in 1985. For a while there were entrenched attitudes from the Merseyside Police, and there was quite a struggle between them and the Chair of the Police Authority, Margaret Simey, who was trying to get a more responsive approach by the police.

> But I think the Scarman Report as well helped that, as did the continuous pressure of the newly established Liverpool 8 Law Centre, and the later work of the Gifford Inquiry in Liverpool, so I think one of the legacies was in due course a less overtly oppressive, racist approach and practice at police level.

Jon Murphy, who is currently the Chief Constable of Merseyside, gives a police perspective on some of the changes that have taken place in policing since 1981:

In some respects things got worse, but that enabled them to get better. They got worse I think because for a while, a very tight triangle was set up called the Toxteth Section, and it was policed in a very different way from the rest of the force. It had lots of police presence, but it was policed in a very defensive aggressive way, if you understand what I mean.

So, if somebody called the police for something, it ... almost became a no go area. It was very difficult for the police to go in there ... and Granby Street in particular became an incredibly difficult place to police ... and the tragedy of that was, there were people in Granby Street who needed the police, and they wanted the police in there, and criminality flourished, and we only came out of that, I guess towards the end of the 8os when we ran some very significant street drug trafficking operations right in the heart of Granby Street ... and they proved to be very successful, and we removed some really good quality criminals if you like, who had been running a very lucrative business, frankly, because the policing of it was not as it should have been because it was so difficult for us to go into. The criminal elements were allowed to flourish. Some of them made a lot of money out of drugs, became very powerful, and they had a very pervasive and negative impact on the communities up there ... and it took a long time to get that back.

But, when we did come out of that, we established a cop shop on Granby Street [4–5 years after the riots], and then we started to build bridges again with the community, and in many respects, we ended up with Toxteth going from one of the worst places in community policing, to being the model, if you like, for the rest of Merseyside Police to engage with communities ... and that cop shop proved hugely successful, hugely successful, and the whole nature of that community changed.

Just after the riots, the first football league match of the season in 1981/2, without doubt the worst violence I've ever seen. But violence has not been a factor in Liverpool football. The club supporters behave themselves really well. But, on that particular match there was definitely an air of 'we can do what we want', and there was a real fight happened, and I was there as well. On Scotland Road, so not even anywhere near Toxteth, there seemed to be this general feeling, 'we can have a fight with the police' ... and the police were baited and goaded, and it ended up in a bit of a pitched battle on Scotland Road ... and I think that was part of a confidence building in the community, actually 'we can fight the police, we can do this' ... and it took a while for that sort of mindset, in some individuals, to be removed.

Today, touch wood, Toxteth gives us very little problems, and we've got really good community relations and interestingly far more multi-cultural than it was then. The neighbourhood that covers that area is what's called E4 to us, but the officers there tell me there's something like 37 or 38 different languages spoken and lots of adults that can't speak English, and the adults [talk] through the children, who learn to speak English in the schools [and translate], and that's how we communicate with the parents. But, there's a really good community policing model up in there, and some of that I think is a legacy of what we had to build, because of what happened in 1981.

There had been continual training [before] the Scarman Report. The whole diversity agenda developed in policing, diversity training, community policing models. I noticed in the report of the Chief Constable as early as September 1981, he doesn't describe it as this, but what we would now call 'community engagement'. As early as September of 81, there is a recognition that actually, if we had built better relationships with these communities, rather than just police them in a particular way, this might not have happened. So, right from the outset there is a recognition that we need to change here ... and that's before Scarman.

It was a seminal moment for British policing ... for British society. It wasn't just about the police, because the police do reflect the society they come from, and some of the stereotypical views that police officers had, some of their attitudes towards race were a direct consequence of their upbringing and the society that they're part of. So, the police, if you like, became a focal point at that particular moment in time, for what was actually going on in broader society, and from that point of view it was a watershed. Not just for policing, but for all of us.

But this police chief's optimism is not shared by all. Gideon Ben-Tovim qualifies his generally positive assessment of changes in policing, quoted above:

However, it is still alarming to read only recently further reports about stop and search, with a hugely disproportionate number of black people being stopped and searched – and ultimately not being charged.

Formal studies of racial biases in stop-and-search practices in Merseyside support Gideon's claims. According to Home Office figures, published in 2000, black people are 7.5 times more likely than white people to be stopped and searched, and 6.5 times more likely to be arrested on Merseyside than whites.[32] Concerns have also been expressed, more generally, about the nature of contact between police and young black men and boys in Toxteth. Shortly before the publication of the Macpherson Report, a spokesperson for the Liverpool 8 Law Centre expressed ongoing dissatisfaction, stating that 'police services are more directed at punitive, rather than preventative, proactive and supportive services towards black people who come into contact

with police officers'.[33] Some others, describing their immediate
experiences of policing, suggest that not enough has changed.
'David', who was 16 when the riots took place, gives a critical
perspective on what has changed and what has not:

> There was a time after the riots where the police were scared
> to approach you. For the first time they didn't want to know
> your name. I never expected that to happen, to finally be left
> alone – marvellous! To be able to do what a majority of people
> do as a matter of fact, to just be able to go about your business.

> You get a cocky attitude from some of them now, because
> they've got like more high-tech equipment. You know,
> extended batons as opposed to, you know, the batons that
> they did have. Better body armour and equipment that
> doesn't burn as well as their predecessors used to. But I feel
> they'll always under-estimate the ingeniousness of the people
> whose rights they are supposed to uphold.

> I wouldn't say it's changed … I think I'd say they've got slimier.
> I believe in the concept of law, but I believe in a concept of
> law that's fair and equal across the board. Not a law that is
> there to serve the needs of the rich social elite, or corporate
> business, because if you look at the law, they're always out
> there defending big business. They're defending those that
> pay the wages. This makes them in my eyes no more than
> state-sponsored mercenaries.

Notes

1   Linton Kwesi Johnson, 'Mekkin Histri', reproduced with permission of the
     author (http://www.lintonkwesijohnson.com/).
2   House of Commons, 6 July 1981. *Hansard*, 1981, pp. 21–30.
3   Worlock and Sheppard, *A Time for Healing*, p. 166.
4   Worlock and Sheppard, *A Time for Healing*, p. 166.
5   M. Young, BBC *Listener Magazine*, 2 November 1978, cited in http://www.
     diversemag.co.uk. Accessed November 2010.
6   W. Nelson, *Black Atlantic Politics: Dilemmas of Political Empowerment in*

Boston and Liverpool (New York: State University of New York Press, 2000), p. 210; cited in D. Whyte, 'Contextualising Police Racism: The Aftermath of the Macpherson Report and the Local Response on Merseyside' (unpublished report, Liverpool John Moores University, June 2002), p. 27.

7 *The Guardian*, 6 July 1981, cited in CARF, 'The Riots', pp. 225–27.

8 Liverpool 8 Defence Committee, 'Why Oxford Must Go', in CARF, 'The Riots', pp. 230–31.

9 Way of the World, *Daily Telegraph*, 14 August 1981.

10 Press Statement by Cllr Mrs Margaret Simey, Chairman, Police Committee, 30.7.81, *Simey Papers*, Liverpool University Special Collections D396/54 (5 boxes).

11 Address to the Police Federation by Mrs Margaret Simey, Chairman of Merseyside Police Committee, 12 November 1981, *Simey Papers*, Liverpool University Special Collections D396/54 (5 boxes).

12 Margaret Simey, diary, 13 November 1981, 'Last night was the AGM of the local [Police] Federation', *Simey Papers*, Liverpool University Special Collections D396/54 (5 boxes).

13 Margaret Simey, Chairman's Report on the work of the Police Authority, 13 September 1982, Confidential [to Labour Group], *Simey Papers*, Liverpool University Special Collections D396/54 (5 boxes).

14 Letter by Ellkan Abrahamson, solicitor, to Mrs Simey, 26 April 1989, enclosing copy of written statement submitted as evidence by Mrs Simey on behalf of [a named individual], *Simey Papers*, Liverpool University Special Collections D396/54 (5 boxes)..

15 CARF, 'The Riots', pp. 230–31.

16 http://news.bbc.co.uk/1/hi/programmes/bbc_parliament/3631579.stma.

17 George Leslie (Baron) Scarman, *The Brixton Disorders 10–12 April 1981: Report of an Inquiry by Lord Scarman*, Cmnd. 8427 (London: HMSO, 1981), pp. 151–52.

18 *Scarman Inquiry Report*, p. 13.

19 *Scarman Inquiry Report*, p. 13.

20 *Scarman Inquiry Report*, p. 45.

21 *Scarman Inquiry Report*, p. 45.

22 A. M. Gifford, Wally Brown and Ruth Bundey, *Loosen the Shackles: First Report of the Liverpool 8 Inquiry into Race Relations in Liverpool* (London: Karia Press, 1989).

23 Liverpool Black Caucus, *The Racial Politics of Militant in Liverpool: The Black Community's Struggle for Participation in Local Politics 1980–1986* (ed. G. Ben-Tovim) (Liverpool: Merseyside Area Profile Group/London: The Runnymede Trust, 1986), pp. 41–42; Gifford, Brown and Bundey, *Loosen the Shackles*, pp. 163–80.

24 Gifford, Brown and Bundey, *Loosen the Shackles*, pp. 22–23, 226.

25 Gifford, Brown and Bundey, *Loosen the Shackles*, pp. 78–80.

26 Gifford, Brown and Bundey, *Loosen the Shackles*, pp. 78–80.
27 Gifford, Brown and Bundey, *Loosen the Shackles*, pp. 82–83.
28 *Scarman Inquiry Report*, pp. 159–61.
29 http://news.bbc.co.uk/1/hi/programmes/bbc_parliament/3631579.stma.
30 *The Guardian*, 'What is Institutional Racism?', http://www.guardian.co.uk, 24 February 1999.
31 Rachel Morris, 'A Summary of The Stephen Lawrence Inquiry' (Cm 4262-l), Report of an Inquiry by Sir William Macpherson of Cluny, Presented to Parliament by the Home Secretary, February 1999, *http://www.law.cf.ac.uk/ tlru/Lawrence.pdf* (last accessed 29 November 2010), p. 2.
32 Whyte, 'Contextualising Police Racism', p. 38.
33 Liverpool 8 Law Centre, 'Response to Merseyside Police Statement', *Racism in the Force* (Liverpool: Liverpool 8 Law Centre, 1998), p. 1.

3

The Inner City

The riots brought Liverpool into the limelight, attracting the national media and a series of high-profile visits by government officials, who addressed Liverpool as a special case but also drew broader conclusion from it, regarding the plight of inner cities. This chapter asks how Toxteth and Liverpool 8 were depicted in media coverage of the riots, then shows how the media also drew a more general picture of these places as examples of inner cities, which were portrayed as problems. The chapter then goes on to examine efforts by organisations and government – including the Church of England and the Conservative government's 'Minister for Merseyside' – to understand and help solve the problems faced by inner cities.

As well as asking how journalists and government officials saw Toxteth and Liverpool, and portrayed this and other inner cities, it is also important to explore the perspectives of residents and community organisations. There was an important difference between these two interpretations of the riots. Whereas the national media and government were keen to explain the riots with reference to social and economic problems experienced by inner cities, local individuals and organisations acknowledged these problems, but were primarily concerned with policing, as Chapter 2 makes clear. Historian P. J. Waller explains:

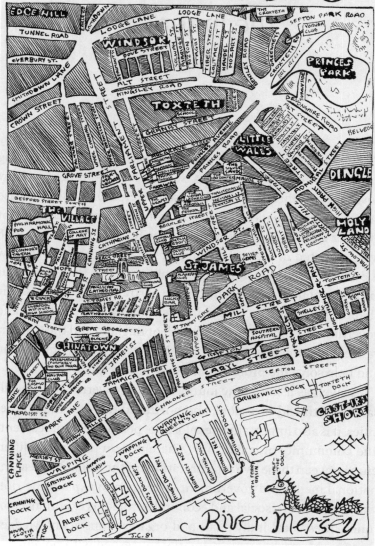

Figure 3.1 'Liverpool 8', by John Cornelius, from *Liverpool 8*
(London: John Murray, 1982).

Black animosity against the police was a central reason for the rioting. That many young whites shared this grievance, that whites subsequently were active in the disturbances and, apparently, even more prominent in the looting, does not negate this statement. The rioting was not a race riot, in that the struggle was not white against black or vice versa; but there was a strong racial component to it, in that rioting would probably never have occurred without the lead being taken by blacks who were aggrieved at police practices. This element was crucial for, as the Secretary of State for the Environment, Michael Heseltine, afterwards saw for himself, Toxteth was not the only deprived area in Liverpool. Slums just as bad – some might say worse, though what meter of misery can pronounce accurately? – exist elsewhere in the city. Netherley, for instance, is a regular embodiment of the hell of modern housing, and the level of unemployment in several Liverpool wards stands at between 33 and 40 per cent. If more emphasis were needed then the Strathclyde region, in and about Glasgow, confirms it. There the air was heavy with desperation through want of work and amenities; nevertheless the region remained silent throughout the summer disturbances. The point is that, though circumstances of multiple economic deprivation were very important pre-conditions of the rioting in Toxteth, they could not alone cause it. Poverty on its own is more likely to extinguish passion than to rouse it, and cumulative misery produces more listlessness, debility, and fatalism than militancy, demonstration, and rebellion.

But, while residents and community organisations stress that the riots were provoked by policing rather than 'inner-city problems', they also acknowledge the latter, and the social and economic stresses experienced in Liverpool 8. This chapter begins by reviewing the ways in which Toxteth and Liverpool 8 were portrayed in national debates – in the media, in the churches, and elsewhere – before asking how local people felt about all this, and how they have expressed their views, both as individuals and also through community organisations.

How the Media Represented Liverpool 8

The media played a powerful role in telling the story of the riots, and in explaining where and why they took place. The first thing journalists did was to label these the 'Toxteth riots'. Claire Dove, who grew up in Liverpool 8, explains the confusion this geographical terminology caused:

> I remember switching on the television to look at the news and they said that there'd been riots in Toxteth in Liverpool. For me and other members of the black community, Toxteth was always Park Road, which was a white area, so I just wondered why people were rioting in Toxteth. Lo and behold, what had actually happened was that it wasn't in Toxteth, it was in Liverpool 8, which was where I came from, Granby. The media needed a tag, a name, and so they used Toxteth, which we never used in our community, and hence they became the notorious Toxteth riots.

Phillip Canter, a solicitor in Liverpool 8, explains why this geographical terminology matters:

> It's always called the Toxteth riots. That's one area in which I have a problem with the general London press. This area in Liverpool was never really called Toxteth by the local people. It was always referred to as Liverpool 8. It is quite clear that somebody came up from London, and saw this sign 'Toxteth' in the area, and ever afterwards they were called the Toxteth riots. But it was Liverpool 8, and always called Liverpool 8, and eventually the Law Centre was set up called the Liverpool 8 Law Centre. It wasn't called the Toxteth Law Centre!

The media then embroidered this picture of Toxteth in sensational detail, again to the irritation of local people. David Copley, the Methodist minister, complains that the press were 'interested in sensation and the whole business about giving [Toxteth] a notorious feel':

> So suddenly something which actually is a perfectly innocent name of a city suburb, whatever it technically is, has suddenly got this cachet of being a horrible name along with Brixton and they suddenly turned everything into something which was seen negatively.

These comments indicate the importance of understanding how the media represented the riots and the area they called 'Toxteth' and, more generally, the 'inner city'. For this, it helps to turn in detail to an analysis of media coverage, provided by cultural geographer Jacquelin Burgess. In the following extract from her chapter 'News from Nowhere' in the 1985 book *Geography, the Media and Popular Culture*, Burgess examines the ways in which newspapers located the riots, and shows that they moved from specific stories to broader pictures of 'inner cities' as generic problem areas.

> In this chapter I examine the ways in which the British national daily papers interpreted the 'riots' of the spring and summer of 1981. How did the media make sense of what happened in the three major conurbations of London, Liverpool and Manchester? For most people, the drama of the events of that year were caught and committed to memory in the form expressed by the mass media.
>
> I discuss the meanings given to the concept of the inner city in the press reports of the disturbances, and argue that the newspapers fulfil an ideological role in which a myth is being perpetuated of *The Inner City* as an alien place, separate

and isolated, located outside white, middle-class values and environments.

I shall analyse texts from a range of national newspapers to explore the meanings given to the localities in which rioting took place. The period covered is April to September 1981, and I used six daily papers – the *Guardian, The Times, Daily Telegraph, Daily Mirror, Daily Star, Daily Mail,* and four Sunday papers – *Observer, The Sunday Times, Sunday Telegraph, Sunday People*. This gives a cross-section of the 'quality' and 'popular' press, covering the current political spectrum.

Newspapers provide both linguistic and visual texts. News itself can be reported in three forms. First, there is the 'factual' reporting of events. Secondly, papers carry special features where, for example, journalists are despatched to places to provide fuller accounts of events. Features also include commissioned articles exploring aspects of the issues (e.g. Beryl Bainbridge on Liverpool 8) and depth analyses which may take a few days to research (e.g. *Daily Star* enquiry into race relations). Thirdly, editorials comment on the news and give voice to the political perspective of the paper. One consequence of this threefold treatment is that particular views are considerably reinforced. Photographs and cartoons provide visual text. Cartoons generally reflect the dominant framework within which news is interpreted. Photographs are designed to be read in association with headline and caption which deeply colours interpretation.

In terms of the selection of photographs and the language used to describe events, there was very little difference between the 'quality' and 'popular' press. Photographs concentrated on the police who were shown in confrontation with white and black people, standing behind riot shields, being led away (bloodied) by colleagues. The aftermath of the riots was portrayed in photographs of burnt-out buildings,

looted shops and damage to property. Very few photographs shared the rioters' perspective, partly because of danger to cameramen and equipment, partly because the opposite visual perspective also offered potential for different interpretations of what was happening.

Riot discourse was a metaphor of war: RIOT TORN, RIOT RAVAGED, THE BATTLE OF BRIXTON, BLOODY SATURDAY, WAR ON THE STREETS. The inner cities were being BLITZED by 'mobs' of young people. Extracting maximum drama from what were already dramatic events, headlines and texts carried extreme emotional tones. Some were blatant, others evoked drama more subtly. Reporters and sub-editors wrote of 'the Toxteth terror, the horror of it all, fear stalking the streets, violence and hate, orgies of looting and violence'. A common description was of the 'anarchic ferocity' of many encounters between police and people. The rioters themselves were supposed 'insane'. The interpretation of the activities of the 'mob' hearkened back to the nineteenth century – 'the rioters were 'irrational, insane, running berserk and losing control'.

Journalists fashion accounts in line with the public voice of their paper and its readership. Take, for example, these two first-hand accounts of Toxteth on the night of Monday 6 July, the first entitled 'A night on both sides of the line', the second 'Bloody battle':

> I was trapped in a council flat as the battle of Upper Parliament Street reached its insane climax just before midnight. Reporters shambled like tramps, removing ties to avoid being identified by looters and attacked. My car was burned out. I escaped down a side street, my eyes stung with CS gas.

> For seven hate-filled hours I ran with the rioters on their rampage of terror. I heard them howling as they drove the

police down Upper Parliament Street and [watched in] horror as the masked men set up a base camp in a tower block and handed out petrol bombs to their frenzied army of teenagers

The style of the two pieces is different but the basic constructions are the same. The criminality of the participants, the insanity of the events, the threat to the reporters and the acceptance of CS gas. In the former, its use is reported 'factually' although linked to the car theft; in the latter it is justified in terms of the 'meagre' armoury of the police. [Others have] argued recently that public acceptance of a militarised police force will probably be the long-lasting impact of the reporting of the riots, because the press were instrumental in changing what had been seen as an exceptional response by the police into one which is a normal and necessary part of crowd control.

The press divided in the extent to which conditions of life in the inner city areas were thought to be causal factors behind the disturbances. Papers such as the *Daily Mail*, *Daily Star*, *Daily* and *Sunday Telegraph* came down firmly on issues of law and order, immigration policies, criminality, lack of parental control and the need to equip the police. These papers were also exercised by the possibilities of a conspiracy. For example, the *Daily Mail* editorial for 9 July 1981 – FIRST CATCH THE RING LEADERS – argued that 'teenage violence is uglier and more destructively anarchic than anything before'. It called for exemplary sentences for offenders and advised the police to turn to the Royal Ulster Constabulary – 'the specialists in contemporary urban terror, for practical advice'. The more 'liberal' press, such as the *Guardian*, *Daily Mirror*, *Observer and Sunday Times* were much more concerned with the 'deprivation' thesis and its associations with government policies. The *Daily Mirror*, for example, in a front-page editorial for 7 July entitled: SAVE OUR CITIES, stressed the immediate necessity of removing the mobs from the streets but went on to argue: 'The smoke that hangs over burning communities is also a pall of despair. The spending on the inner cities has been ruthlessly and blindly cut ... The riots, the racial attacks, the tensions and the intolerance have social causes and political solutions'. None, however, supported the actions of the people who took to the streets.

The Myth of the Inner City: Four separate domains contribute to the inner city myth by weaving together the streets, shops and houses, the empty spaces, the different cultural styles, class and racial characteristics, legitimate and 'illegitimate' forms of behaviour. The place which is created is empty of reality. The inner city is alien, outside 'normal' places. It is populated by white and black people who are outside 'normal' society. Both the inner city and its inhabitants threaten the values and standards of 'civilised society'. A *Daily Mirror* piece about Toxteth before the riots illustrates the way in which the myth is constructed. Four grainy black and white photographs complete this picture: one depicting a bloodied policeman, the others showing different views of 'derelict' Toxteth: a vandalised, burnt-out car carries reminders of the riot photographs; the men sitting on the ledge of a boarded-up, crumbling mansion convey ideas of what Toxteth once was before the collapse of 'civilised' life; the posed picture with the two little girls is a romanticised comment on 'racial harmony'. The text is sparse, direct and conveys enough information for its readers to grasp the essential meaning of Toxteth and the inner city, which is described as 'virtually a black ghetto':

THIS is the grim face of Toxteth, Liverpool 8 – the rundown area which became front-page news after a weekend of savage rioting. These pictures specially taken for the Daily Mirror in March show the squalor and desolation of what was once a middle-class suburb.

An editorial in *The Times* is a more complex text but creates the same understanding. Entitled SOUND THE ALARM, the paper expresses great concern for the younger generation who 'have to live in the decaying inner cities, from where the more able, the more self sufficient, the more ambitious have quit, leaving behind less fortunate and the inadequate. Their housing is often substandard; they live in vandalised tower blocks or soul-less estates ... any community life there may have been has broken down'. The editorial blames poor educational facilities, bad teachers and the lack of parental control for the production of these inadequate people. It suggests that blacks have additional burdens because of discrimination. In consequence, young people are 'rootless, jobless, alienated from their parents' generation, resentful of the deal they are getting from society'. The editorial concludes that both white and black young people 'find excitement in crime, in violence, in fighting authority first with attitudes, then with stones ... ' The newspaper does not connect feelings of alienation and resentment with the street disturbances. It interprets those actions as a desire for 'excitement' rather than as a valid political protest.

'*The Derelict Terraces and Rundown Tatty Streets*': The language of the built environment is limited. A few adjectives and stock phrases are used to describe all three localities: rundown, decaying, derelict, dilapidated, shabby and sleazy. Upper Parliament Street was described as 'a desolate shambles of rundown Victorian houses and modem tenement slums'; Liverpool 8 as 'a sprawling hatch of rundown houses and shops'. 'Rundown' is ubiquitous and carries two meanings; first, of unsightliness and second of neglect. 'The dilapidated rundown shops are as unsightly as ever'. Rundown as neglect reflects either on the activities of residents or the policies of the local authority. In Toxteth, Heseltine apparently saw 'the self inflicted wounds of people who have vandalised their own housing estates, brought terror and anarchy to their own streets'. Most papers preferred the easier target of local authority policy, which accorded more directly with readers' commonsense understanding. Rundown means planning blight, or the failure to complete schemes because the money ran out.

The built environments of Brixton and Toxteth offered considerable scope for emotive, 'creative' features which relied on the stereotypes of slum life and public housing. Charles Laurence, writing in the *Sunday Telegraph* introduces Toxteth in A TALE OF TWO CITIES:

> It is the sort of area where it is hard to tell the riot damage from the urban decay. Rows of grimy back-to-backs, some lived in, others heaps of rubble and charred timber are punctuated by stark modern flats and stretches of waste ground. There is graffiti everywhere.

The Inner City: That representative of The Establishment, *The Times* newspaper offers its readers a chilling reminder of what can happen when 'the mob' breaks loose:

> Toxteth presented an awful picture of anarchy. We saw looters of all ages, and both sexes, black and white. The savagery of the pitched battle ... went beyond anything that most experienced observers had seen before. The mob screamed, the buildings roared in flames [amidst] the sound of shouting and laughter ...

The empty, hollow form of the myth 'locates' inner cities as distinct, separate, alien and potentially destructive of 'our civilised way of life'. The myth removes the places and the people who live in them to a grey, shabby, derelict, poverty-ridden fairytale-land which can be conveniently ignored because it has no reality.

National attention to inner cities, which this kind of media coverage informed and provoked, was advanced through a series of practical interventions. The most important of these was the Prime Minister's decision to send Michael Heseltine (the Secretary of State for the Environment) to Liverpool, where he was to investigate the economic, social and environmental problems of that city. This meant confronting challenging but ultimately localised issues, and thereby pushing fundamental questions about racism and the legitimacy of policing out of sight. As explained in Chapter 5, it also brought the response to the riots back onto Conservative home ground, with the assertion that a market would ultimately be found, and that only this could bring Liverpool back from the brink. But the inner-city agenda was not always so narrow or evasive. For others, it signalled a commitment to supporting members of marginalised and excluded communities, as well as the continued commitment of existing activists through community-based organisations, as the final section in this chapter explains.

Faith in the City

Building on the cooperation between Catholics and Anglicans during the riots (discussed in Chapter 1), faith groups reaffirmed their commitment to the communities and areas affected by the riots. The most tangible expression of this was *Faith in the City*, a report and plan of action published by the Church of England. In his autobiography, *Steps Along Hope Street*, which was published in 2002, David Sheppard looked back on *Faith in the City*, reflecting that it had achieved a high profile, not least because the government and some of its allies in the media disliked it so much. Two days before its publication, the *Sunday Times* front page headline read: 'Church report is Marxist'. The article quoted a 'senior government figure' who described sections of the report as 'pure Marxist theology'. This was contested in other sections of the media, notably the *Financial Times*, but the story stayed on the front pages for four days, raising the profile of the report nationally. The following extracts illustrate the tone of the report, showing how lessons were learned from Liverpool and other cities, and thus how the riots in Liverpool informed a national understanding of inner-city problems, and an agenda for solving these problems, through the established Church.

This built upon the agenda, examined by Jacquelin Burgess in relation to the media, which drew general conclusions from specific experiences and events, learning broad lessons from localised riots. Liverpool featured prominently in Anglican reflection on the riots, and this is evident in the 'popular version' of *Faith in the City*, an accessible summary of the full report, which was illustrated with photographs of Toxteth.[1] *Faith in the City* defines Urban Priority Areas (UPAs), which are 'places of absolute poverty, of the relative poverty which is integral to an unequal society, and of increasing poverty by comparison with national norms and the favoured minority of middle Britain: this has to be termed polarization'.[2] These areas exhibit three forms of decline: economic, physical and social. This report does not blame the fate of UPAs upon their inhabitants, but upon the wider social and economic order, and it asserts that 'there is a collective responsibility for the problems of poverty and inequality that we have described'.[3] *Faith in the City* concentrated on poverty and inequality rather than racism or policing, but its agenda was progressive, asserting a conception of justice with renewed regard for 'the protection of the poor, the weak and the vulnerable',[4] and arguing for a critical approach to law and order, not simply stronger policing:

> In UPAs we have found a widespread ambivalence towards the agents of 'the Law' (particularly the police and magistrates).

On the one hand the Law is seen as the guardian of the status quo and the protector of the weaker members of the community against the stronger; but on the other hand the status quo itself is felt to be oppressive, and the agents of the Law often appear to be prejudiced against certain classes of people. Black people, for example, must look to the police for protection, not only against burglars, but also against physical attacks and thuggery carried out by racist or extreme political groups; but they may also have personal experiences (such as the feeling that the police take no notice of calls coming from areas where they are known to live), and have heard utterances of police spokesmen, which make them believe that the police are prejudiced against them. We have received so many reports of this kind that we cannot discount them. This loss of confidence in the police, and suspicion of racial or class discrimination in methods of policing and among magistrates, can result in substantial groups in the community ceasing to regard the Law as 'friend'.[5]

Evangelical Responses to the Riots

The Anglicans were not the only Christians to reflect on the problems and prospects of inner cities in the wake of the riots, of course. *Faith in the City* acknowledged that membership of the Church of England was declining in 'Urban Priority Areas', though it did not accept that this decline was irreversible, and observed that participation in other churches was stronger. It specifically cited evangelical churches, which attracted congregations from within the black communities. The wider set of Christian responses to the riots, introduced in Chapter 1, included reflections on the inner-city areas in which the churches were and are active. An important contribution in this context was a study commissioned by the Evangelical Coalition for Urban Missions, by Michael G. LeRoy. *Riots in Liverpool 8:*

Some Christian Responses (1983) was introduced as 'the closest there has been to a Scarman Report into the 1981 riots in Liverpool 8', explaining that it 'focuses on the evangelical churches of Liverpool 8 and their responses to these events'.[6] The study found that there were about forty churches in Liverpool 8 including four that were particularly large and growing. It found that '[d]uring the riots Christians played a small, but sometimes significant role as mediators, peacemakers, communicators, proclaimers, helpers, carers and protectors' and that these roles included providing counselling and support for those most directly affected.[7] LeRoy argued that churches had made some clumsy attempts to understand the riots and sympathise with the tensions that underpinned them. Officers of the British Council of Churches (BCC), he notes, 'visited the area for a couple of days' and made the controversial decision to send £500 to the Liverpool 8 Defence Committee, money that was used to 'ferry families and friends to see those in custody' following the wave of arrests that accompanied the riots. Though other organisations including the Methodist Youth Club had supported the same cause, some church members were 'outraged' by the BCC's intervention. This prompted the organisation to look for other ways of supporting the Liverpool 8 communities.

> As the dust of the BCC grant issue settled, church leaders called for a specific way of showing their concern for Liverpool 8. It soon became evident that Liverpool 8's lack of a Law Centre to provide free legal advice and representation was a central issue. Local people remained deeply suspicious of the 'establishment' and so looked for support elsewhere. Local authority patronage of Law Centres in other cities ... was seen to be undesirable, so the Law Centre Working Party turned to the churches for help. The main denominations committed themselves to a 'partnership of trust between the

churches and the local community' and to financial support
for at least five years.[8]

A building for this organisation was found and the centre
opened in 1982 on Princes Road. LeRoy acknowledges this
positive move, but also highlights the broader set of problems
which it raised. Acknowledging the bigger story of urban Britain,
exposed in Toxteth, LeRoy's report paints a picture 'in which
most social institutions are shaking – the family, law, economy
and education':[9]

> Liverpool 8 is, in many senses, a microcosm of the issues
> at the heart of Britain's present ill-health. The riots raised
> questions of law and authority, they revealed the weakness
> of politics, brought into the open racial and class antago-
> nism, they happened in an inner city area exemplifying the
> problems of mass, one-class housing associated with high
> unemployment, and in the aftermath local schools experi-
> enced the backwash of local feeling.[10]

Changing Perceptions of Toxteth and Liverpool 8

Though sections of the media, church and even the Conservative government were well-meaning in their efforts to identify
and solve the problems of inner-city areas such as Liverpool 8,
residents of these places were not so happy to be portrayed as
problems, and they pointed out that being labelled a 'no-go' area
was both insulting and bad for business. Derek Murray, who
was Assistant Warden at the Caribbean Centre, reflects on the
negative consequences of having a Liverpool 8 postcode: 'if you
had a Liverpool 8 address, and it applied I think to both black
and white, [there was no point] applying for a job'. There 'was
very much a perception that Liverpool 8 was used as a dumping
ground' for 'undesirable families'.

Some residents and supporters of these areas have responded by challenging negative stereotypes and trying to put
more positive ones in their places. In Liverpool, this rejection of
labels began with geographical terminology. The media rushed
to locate the riots in Toxteth, whereas they were actually spread
more widely, reaching into Granby, and it would have been
more accurately to speak of Liverpool 8. Newspapers routinely
referred to 'Toxteth, the well-known riot centre' (*Daily Telegraph*,
14 August 1981), whereas locals insisted on speaking of Liverpool
8, a term which remained free of negative associations. The
writer and illustrator John Cornelius challenged negative
stereotypes with positive pictures and stories about Liverpool
8, first published in 1982. Two of his line drawings, including a
whimsical map of Liverpool 8 and a diverse and lively shopping
scene, are reproduced in Figures 3.1 and 3.2. Perhaps ironically,
when Liverpool came to sell itself to the world through City
of Culture 2008, it chose precisely this kind of image for its
slogan – 'The World in One City' – which reclaimed diversity.
This can be understood as part of a broader attempt to present
Liverpool in a positive light, and finally extinguish the negative
images that media coverage of the riots had helped fix in the
national imagination. A survey of investors conducted in 2008
had found that the city's reputation was still shaped by social
and political problems dating from the 1980s. As one put it, 'I
think Liverpool still does carry that tag that it's had since the
'70s, it's not necessarily seen as a good place to come, ... people
remember the Toxteth riots'. Some investors added, however,
that they believed the city's negative reputation would be
changed by the City of Culture, and the sustained good publicity
that would bring.[11]

Residents challenged negative pictures of Liverpool 8 and
put forward some positive stories about their neighbourhood.

'Out shopping'

Figure 3.2 'Out shopping', by John Cornelius, from *Liverpool 8* (London: John Murray, 1982).

These comments appeared on an internet forum:

> There are just too many generalisations about L8. The communities here are diverse. There is still a lot of poverty but there is a sense, too, that things are changing for the better. New communities are moving in, and on the whole we rub along together well enough.[12]

> I went to school in L8 during the riots and have lived in Falkner Square for the past 5 years. It's a beautiful cosmopolitan area where the houses are selling like hot cakes as the area is restored back to its original grandeur. Okay there's the odd scally around causing mischief but on the whole this area of Toxteth is on the up. 13

Derek Murray elaborates on this positive picture of Liverpool 8, recalling the area as he first saw it in the early 1970s:

> If you take that first day that I arrived at Liverpool 8, the biggest thing that struck me walking down the street was, suddenly there's all these people that look like me. Not only do they look like me, right, but they nod to me, right, as if they know me. They acknowledge me. That's very odd, yeah. So, there is a sense of brotherhood, you know ... and that still goes on to a lesser extent there. So, there was a level of acceptance there.

Murray qualifies this picture of Liverpool 8 by acknowledging that his feelings towards the area have been mixed – he uses the term 'ambiguous' – and that the reality is more positive than outsiders have often claimed, if not wholly positive. In other words, in this as in any area, there has been room for improvement, not only in policing but in some other areas too. Those who know what these problems are, and how best to solve them, are likely to be local residents and community groups, as the next section explains.

Community Organisations

Before, during and after the riots, a number of community organisations represented local people and asserted their needs and wishes, which began with better policing and extended to social, economic and political issues such as anti-discrimination practices in the City Council and private sector. In the following interview, community activist and academic Gideon Ben-Tovim introduces some of these organisations, many of which are referred to throughout this book, and explains how they sought to represent the people of Liverpool 8, including members of the Liverpool-born black community:

> The Community Relations Council (CRC) was quite an impor-
> tant body because it was semi-statutory and with a diverse
> and representative membership. It was an umbrella body that
> brought together ethnic minority organisations, the volun-
> tary sector, the churches, the local authority, trade unions
> and political parties. It became quite active all through the
> 70s and 80s, and people who were involved in the Commu-
> nity Relations Council were also involved in establishing
> Merseyside Anti-Racialist Alliance (MARA) at the end of the
> 1970s.
>
> Some who were involved in the CRC or MARA also formed
> the Liverpool Black Organisation (LBO), which was an impor-
> tant body representing the Liverpool-born black community.
> There was also several important centres for the community:
> the Charles Wootton Centre for Education, the Caribbean
> Centre, the Pakistan Centre, the Hindu Centre, whilst the
> Methodist Centre was a very significant place where young
> black people felt free and able to go in safely and in comfort,
> which wasn't the case in most of the other youth facilities
> in and around Liverpool 8 and the city centre. The Afro-
> Asian Caribbean Standing Committee was another body that

brought together some of the traditional minority organisations in an umbrella group.

Such organisations rallied together around shared local concerns of racism and discrimination but also saw links to wider national and even international struggles. These groups came together around demonstrations, marches, and campaigns. This was a very active period, and the links between those various different organisations brought together people from the community as well as the University [Area Profile Group].

There were many shared agendas then: people working together within different organisations ... There was the growing agenda nationally around the Race Relations Act. Race and community relations were becoming increasingly 'hot' issues in the 1970s. These included the Free Angela Davis campaign and Rock Against Racism. There were others of course: the women's movement, CND and the peace movement, the student movement, anti-apartheid, Chile Solidarity, and Vietnam.

In Liverpool there was then a pretty active period of anti-racism all through the 1970s. A lot of mobilisation, engagement, and campaigning, and many demands on the political structure for change, based on the degree of exclusion of people from the black community from some of the key institutions: education, housing, social services, employment and the political system; and at the heart of the concerns, and of the eventual disturbances, was the issue around the racist policing of the community.

We pointed out the dangers of where the level of alienation, discrimination and disadvantage could lead to. After the events in Bristol and Brixton, there was clearly the potential for outbreaks of serious disorder in Liverpool, in that there had been a big build-up of tension around policing issues all through the 1970s.

So, though he joined most other 'insiders' in stressing that policing was by far the single most important issue for residents and communities of Liverpool 8, this commentator also acknowledged that broader issues of alienation, discrimination and disadvantage were also at play. These issues, rather than policing, were the focus of the Conservative government's response to the riots, discussed in Chapter 5. First, though, there is more to say about the communities who participated in and were affected by these events, including a vulnerable and disadvantaged group who were particularly involved: children and young people, whose experiences are examined in Chapter 4.

Notes

1   Archbishop of Canterbury's Commission on Urban Priority Areas, *Faith in the City: A Call for Action by Church and Nation*, The Report of the Archbishop of Canterbury's Commission on Urban Priority Areas (London: Church House Publishing, 1985).
2   *Faith in the City*, p. 24.
3   *Faith in the City*, p. 24.
4   *Faith in the City*, p. 328.
5   *Faith in the City*, pp. 338–39.
6   Michael G. LeRoy, *Riots in Liverpool 8: Some Christian Responses* (research report commissioned, printed and distributed by the Evangelical Coalition for Urban Mission, London, 1983), p. v.
7   LeRoy, *Riots in Liverpool 8*, p. x.
8   LeRoy, *Riots in Liverpool 8*, pp. 81–83.
9   LeRoy, *Riots in Liverpool 8*, p. 100.
10 LeRoy, *Riots in Liverpool 8*, p. 99.
11 David O'Brien, 'Who Pays the Piper? Understanding the Experience of Organisations Sponsoring the Liverpool European Capital of Culture', report, October 2008, edited by Impacts 08, http://www.liv.ac.uk/impacts08/Papers/Impacts08(Oct08)WhoPaysThePiper-SponsorReport.pdf.
12 http://www.bbc.co.uk/liverpool/content/articles/2006/06/28/toxteth_anniversary_feature.shtm.
13 http://www.bbc.co.uk/liverpool/content/articles/2006/06/28/toxteth_anniversary_feature.shtm.

Figure 1.1 Milk float (Upper Parliament St, junction of Kingsley Rd). Photograph by Goff Tinsley, with permission. Jon Murphy, then a police constable in Liverpool 8, remembers 'the dairy on Upper Parliament Street being set on fire, the milk floats being brought out [and] driven at the police line'.

Figure 1.2 Barricades (Upper Parliament St). Photograph by Goff Tinsley, with permission.

Figure 2.1 Police shields and dog (Upper Parliament St). Photograph by Goff Tinsley, with permission.

Figure 4.1 After the riots (Lodge Lane). Photograph by Goff Tinsley. Notice the Royal Wedding images displayed in the shop window; this was also the year of Charles and Diana's wedding.

Figure 4.2 Children exploring after the riot. Photograph by Goff Tinsley.

Figure 5.1 The Rialto (Upper Parliament St) was burned down during the riots. Photograph by Goff Tinsley, with permission.

Figure 5.2 The Rialto thirty years later, rebuilt as part of a housing development. Photograph by and with permission of Donnamarie Barnes and Mike Boyle, 2010.

Figure 5.3 Lodge Lane Regeneration Zone, 2010. Photograph by and with permission of Donnamarie Barnes with Mike Boyle.

Figure 5.4 Site of the Garden Festival, 2010. Photograph by and with permission of Donnamarie Barnes with Mike Boyle, 2010.

Figure 6.1 Dome and spire illustrating the changing ethnic and social profile of Granby. Photograph by and with permission of Donnamarie Barnes with Mike Boyle, 2010.

4

Young People and Education

Many of those involved in the riots were children and young people. Some were still at school, and others might have been students at nearby universities, had the education system served them better. Goff Tinsley's photographs of the aftermath of the riots show children picking their way through damaged shops and rubble-strewn streets, playing and exploring (Figures 4.1, 4.2). Some of the oral histories of the riots, quoted throughout this book, describe experiences of people who were barely in their teens when the riots took place. This chapter explores the wider context and legacy of these young people's experiences, beginning with stories of police harassment and going on to focus on education.

Young people were directly involved in the riots. Wally Brown remembers a mixture of 'young people' and 'some older people' on the streets. Some were out to 'settle old scores' and others were 'young kids'. 'David,' who was 16 at the time, explains that it was not just the old who had scores to settle. He reflects on his experiences of the police when growing up in the Dingle:

> I'd constantly be stopped because I lived in a white area and generally I would be stopped on the basis of 'What are you doing here?' They'd stop you on your bike. I remember one night, one night in particular, I got stopped on me bike the

top of Warwick Street by an old Irish Guards cadet building. They gave me such a hard time, that honestly by the time they had finished I felt like I had robbed my own bike! The usual 'Where are you going? Is this your bike? What's your serial number? Give us your serial number' ... I remember that being a traumatic experience.

Or when they'd literally make you take your shoes and socks off in the street. Now, you could go and relay that story to people, about how you could be stopped and the police could convince you that they were entitled by law to make you take your shoes off. [They'd say] 'You can do it here or at the station.' People who have never experienced this would find it unbelievable. I mean, it's ironic that later when the Miners' Strike was on, people actually seen the police for what they were.

But, you know, to go and tell your parents that this has happened to you, was it seems always met with the same response: 'Oh, you must have done something' ...

There were a few white lads that were known to the police, they would also be questioned, but predominantly, it would be the black or the racial minority amongst them that would be getting the hard time or worse still, being picked up and arrested.

But these were the kind of things that were happening to us and if it wasn't us it would be your brothers or other friends' families that would be the ones getting dragged into jeeps and stuff. People who you'd know, you'd be playing with them one minute and the next time you'd see them, they'd be black and blue and you'd known they'd have got a hiding because you were the last person to see them and they weren't covered in bruises. But, try going in front of a magistrate or a setting such as that and relaying details of what had happened to you. You got to a situation where any respect you may have had, had by this time totally disappeared. It got that way that you began to detest them as being overpaid tosspots who abuse their respective positions. We no longer feared them ...

Stories of the riots, told by people who were very young at the time, tend to blend into stories of police harassment, but they also paint a broader picture of life in Liverpool 8. This is largely a picture of disadvantage, in which children and young people are let down by poor schools and are excluded from the advantages of a good education. One of the more positive legacies of the riots has been an acknowledgement of educational problems, motivating a series of attempts to resolve them. Before turning to education, it is also important to acknowledge some institutions that were serving children and the young better.

One important focal point for young people in the area was the Methodist Youth Centre on Princes Road. David Copley, then the Methodist Minister, remembers how this club reached out to the Granby community, offering 'a place where it was safe to go'. It attracted hundreds of young people, most of whom were black or mixed-race, and who used this as a meeting place and cultural centre. David Copley explains:

One of the things that struck me ... was that there were members of the Youth Centre in their mid-twenties. Why? Of course, there was nothing else, so this place developed as a sort of place for teenagers as they grew beyond teen age into their early twenties because there was nowhere else where they were accepted or felt accepted or felt they belonged. The Methodist Centre had become a cultural, social, educational and sports facility.

The Youth Centre features prominently in stories of the riots, told by people who were young at the time. Michael Simon, who was 13 at the time and lived off Granby Street, gives a sense of how the Centre provided a safe space, albeit one hemmed in by police and by an anxious journey home:

> If you can imagine, [the Methodist youth club finishes at] 10.00pm and you'd get the kids spreading out in every direction, you'd always get an incident coming from there, you'd always get someone pulled up further up the avenue, the police would never bother anyone *per se* there because there was too many kids but further up and further down, you'd always hear incidents of that. I can remember in them days we used to travel through ... the alleyways just to avoid the police of a night and this happened all the time, or ran to places, just to avoid them, that was the kind of conditions we were living under.

Wally Brown, who was a youth worker, tells a similar story:

> We used to have a disco on a Thursday night at the Methodists, and all the black kids from Liverpool would go there, and we were there till 10 o'clock. A lot of the kids lived across from the Methodists. They all lived on the Berkeley Estate, so they had to go across the Boulevard, and as you know with Liverpool, you've got the Princes Road, Princes Avenue and a wide Boulevard there ... and the police used to have a habit of parking the Land Rover on the Boulevard just before the kids come out. They would do that regularly ... and the kids would have to come back to us and say 'Would you do us a favour? Stand here and watch us walking across the Boulevard so the police don't get us.' Now, there's young people asking us to protect them, walking across from the police, and the police are supposed to be protecting them.

Young People and Education

In 1978 the Methodist Youth Centre put in an application for funding to build a library. The Minister, David Copley, explains that they did so because they were 'concerned about ... education, supplementary education for kids who were generally not achieving at school'. This reflected a more widespread feeling that schools, colleges and universities were failing young people in Liverpool 8, and that this contributed to their deprivation and exclusion. This was a feeling shared by children themselves. Michael Simon, who was 13, puts this succinctly: school, he says, 'was shit':

> In the summer of '81, I was 13, so I was in senior school and I was in Shorefields ... which at the time was a really big school, the pupils were predominantly from the Liverpool 8 area and particularly from the Granby Street area, in other words it was the biggest racially mixed school within Liverpool at the time.

> [School] was shit, I didn't learn a thing, I was just totally lost. Actually I think I was suspended something like 13 times ... it was because I answered teachers back basically, which I was proud of at the time.

> It just so happened that most of the bottom groups were definitely full of all the black lads, definitely, lads who I grew up with, I got immediately put in there and when they'd suspend me, I'd just say it's too easy, they gave me a test ... I passed my 11 plus but I didn't learn another thing in school. At that time, Shorefields was just a waste of time for any black kid that went there and the school were aware of that.

> Not that you see many overt, if you like, racist acts by the teachers, but there was an undercurrent definitely about who was singled out for things [and] who wasn't. You look back

and you know why there were so many black kids [in the bottom groups].

You also had schools closing down, [like the one at the end of Lodge Lane], all these local schools and I still think that's got something to do with the education system as it is now in Liverpool 8. The schools were kind of like tapering off an there was no investment in them, I'm guessing that no-one went to school above 14 at that time and kind of, maybe they might have been stuck in that kind of mode [...] but there was no jobs was there? And I think government schemes were coming in, what was it called, Opportunities Programme? No-one was getting a job and when I think about it now, maybe that was three years before [the riots], it was already a given there was no jobs and there were these schemes which no-one liked to go on anyway, even at the time. Most of the black kids within Shorefields [felt] what's the use, what's the point?

Derek Murray, who worked at the Caribbean Centre, tells a similar story:

Certainly at the time, education was an issue. The quality of the schools was an issue. The quality of the teaching was an issue ... employment prospects were very difficult.

So, job opportunities were [poor] ... well, I think first of all educational attainment was very low, noticeably low. Shockingly low, in many respects ... Youth unemployment, I think, was the thing that really stood out from all the things that I was working in, and that was certainly in terms of the broader community efforts that I was involved with on behalf of the Caribbean Centre. It was really about looking at ways that we could begin to kind of in some way address the youth employment situation ... because it was absolutely shameful. I mean, the figures were shocking. 70% or more youth unemployment ... and I believe [that] even if you look back to when we made the two films twenty years on, there hadn't been that much inroads into some of those figures, I believe. But significant inroads had been made by then into educational attainment.

Prior to the riots, I'd been involved in an organisation called Total Play, and we actually had a bunch of kids from Liverpool 8 working with us. It was one of the early job creation programmes. We had a bunch of mostly black or mixed race kids from Liverpool 8, and we were working up in the north end of the city, in the Victoria settlement, and ... that was unusual. That was regarded as very unusual. So, there was also this sort of [thinking that] black people weren't expected to be functioning outside of Liverpool 8.

Mike Boyle, who grew up in Liverpool 8, looks back on the educational experiences of people in Liverpool 8 from the 1950s and 1960s:

Black school leavers of the early sixties ... faced an even bleaker prospect of securing any form of employment that offered any kind of social advancement; not only did they have a poor educational experience to overcome, they also had to combat discrimination and structural racism in employment that was very much a feature of this port city. Clearly therefore the problems faced by blacks living in the Princes Park and Granby area were very much an historic feature of the black experience in Liverpool. [This experience] blighted and stunted the social and economic growth of generations of black people.

Some schools in the area were marginally better than others but the fact remains most were nothing more than repositories for failure for the vast majority of pupils, both black and white.

The apparent poor performance of the area's schools at both primary and junior level condemned many of the pupils to an education at secondary school level which at best was ill-equipped to challenge and stretch the pupils educationally.

Gideon Ben-Tovim summarises the problem:

Local people from the community on the whole were not getting through education and into higher education except where parents were able to give exceptional levels of support and direction to their children, and had outstanding skills to navigate the social system, despite the countervailing pressures they were facing and the institutional second-class citizenship that was being offered.

The Swann Report:
The Educational Needs of 'Liverpool Blacks'

By the time rioting erupted in Liverpool and other cities in 1981, Lord Swann had already begun a major Inquiry into the Education of Children from Ethnic Minority Groups, but he was able to widen the terms of his investigation in response to the disturbances. In particular, he included a valuable chapter on the 'Liverpool blacks', a group of black and minority ethnic residents of Liverpool, most of whom were longstanding residents of the city, who were not themselves immigrants, who could trace family backgrounds in the Caribbean and West Africa, and who lived in Liverpool 8. Lord Swann identified this group as one of the most excluded within the UK's education system. This depressing picture was tempered only by Swann's positive agenda, set out in the interests of engagement, inclusion and educational advancement.

We have included 'Liverpool Blacks' in our report for two reasons. Firstly, this group has probably, we believe, fared worse than any other we have described, with the exception of travellers, in its educational and career achievements, and therefore has a particularly strong claim to the consideration and positive action which we hope will arise out of our findings. Secondly, and paradoxically, this group appears to be more closely assimilated with the ' majority' by ancestry, language, culture, and length of residence than any of the others we have looked at. Its experiences therefore lead us to ask new questions, both about this particular group itself and about many of the accepted assumptions concerning ethnicity.

Definition of Liverpool Blacks: There is a long-established community in Liverpool of African, mixed African and English, or African and Liverpool-Irish-descent, with some of Asian descent as well. The mixed community characteristic of the modern city grew from the end of the nineteenth century onwards, mainly through the settlement of African seamen. By the late 1940s the ethnic minority population of Liverpool was recorded as coming mainly from West Africa and the West Indies. It is this group of long-established families that we call 'Liverpool Blacks'. Many are blood relations of Liverpool 'whites' and have 'black' grandparents and great-great parents born in Liverpool; they speak 'scouse' with a vocabulary, grammar and intonation identical with those of 'white' Liverpudlians, and in short there is nothing but their colour and hapless situation to distinguish them from other long-established residents. However, there has been a tendency to lump them together with relatively recent 'immigrants', in the strict sense of the word, who have been born abroad, especially those who are non white. Characteristic of 'white' Liverpudlian comments are: 'I don't know which are West Indians. They're just white or coloured' or 'We don't have immigrants here, just coloured.' People speaking of 'Liverpool Blacks' sometimes mean only the long established group and sometimes, a larger and more varied set of people. This confusion makes it difficult to give an accurate estimate of the size of the Liverpool Black population: We have received estimates varying from 20,000 to 45,000. It has been estimated by Merseyside Community Relations Council that roughly half the racial minority population of the city are Liverpool Blacks under the terms of our broad definition.

Location of Group: The great majority of Liverpool Blacks live in Liverpool 8, near the city centre. The Anglican and Roman Catholic cathedrals are both situated here as is the University. It includes broad and beautiful streets, once the place of handsome residences which have now 'gone to seed': fine houses stand empty, their facades deteriorating. The most notable landmark to be burnt down in the 1981 disturbances was the Rialto, which had once been a dance-hall that refused admission to 'coloureds' and had later been transformed into a factory that did not employ them. Liverpool 8 also houses a 'white' population, largely Irish, and as a whole is marked by poverty and lack of opportunity.

It was suggested in evidence to us that: 'Liverpool in the 1980s is a sort of model of what British cities in general may be like in the early 2000s, when the majority of 'immigrants' will not be immigrants at all but British-born.' The city was once very prosperous, but its prosperity, based initially on slavery and sugar, then on shipping and colonial trade, has been declining throughout the present century. The silent docks, waste factory sites and decaying warehouses are a graphic picture of the end of the era of Britain's industrial and commercial dominance; the recession arrived in Liverpool long before it hit most of the country, and many witnesses suggested that other major cities would look just like it in another 20 years' time. Unemployment is the overriding problem. There are men in their 40s in Liverpool who have never had a job, and never expect to. On a visit in 1982, one of our members asked a primary school Head how many of the children's parents were unemployed, and received in reply a look of surprise and the answer: 'Oh, there's not many here *working*.' It was clear from the secondary schools visited that school leavers face grave difficulty in obtaining any employment.

Appalling though the situation is for all Liverpudlians, it is markedly worse for the ethnic minorities than for 'whites', and has been so throughout living memory. In the 1930s, a group of 'white' professionals calling themselves the Association for the Welfare of Half-Caste Children, reconstituted in 1937 as the Liverpool Association for the Welfare of Coloured People, appointed a research worker to investigate a range of problems, including employment. Of 119 firms approached, 45 said they would not employ coloured people, and 63 did not reply. (The Association thought the only way to deal with this situation was to stop the settlement of colonial seamen in Liverpool and to consider returning African British subjects to their native countries.)

Education: The 1973 Report of the Select Committee on Race Relations and Immigration on education 1 criticised Liverpool's education system as it found that the Black community was disadvantaged both inside and outside school. Liverpool was criticised for its inability to provide a lead to other LEAs with substantial ethnic minority populations. In the words of the Select Committee's report: '*Liverpool... left us with a profound sense of uneasiness.*' The Report of the 1980/1981 Home Affairs Committee expressed similar concerns about the City's educational provision and practice.

In our visits to various primary and secondary schools in Liverpool 8, we were struck by the teachers' perception of the uncertainty facing their schools. The Heads and their senior colleagues were serving in 'acting' capacities whilst the LEA considered various re-organisation options. Despite individual commitment by a number of teachers, the lack of clear policy by the Authority seemed to leave teachers without a sense of direction. It is interesting that the HMI Report in March 1982 acknowledged that teachers, especially in primary schools, were trying to establish caring environments even though standards of pupil achievement were not high: 'HMI have seen work that is soundly prepared and shows the dedication of the teachers but it is often limited in range and its expectations of pupils ... the low attainments noted appear, in some measure, to be a result of low expectations on the part of teachers, parents and the pupils themselves.'

In addition to a general failure in educational performance, HMI also noted considerable social aggression between pupils, discipline problems, truancy and cynicism among pupils about examination courses and MSC opportunities. The Report also criticised the LEA for mismanagement, lack of clear guidelines for schools, instability of staffing and low teacher morale, and narrow curriculum policies with few initiatives and commented on: '... the apparent inability of elected members to agree on, or pursue any, positive responses to many of the major problems ... leading to feelings of insecurity and uncertainty in every institution and area of the education service.'

Difficulties have been exacerbated by rapidly falling school rolls and the growing number of small secondary schools has had serious consequences for the curriculum. In the smallest schools some subjects, such as Music and some Modern Languages, have been phased out and others are threatened. Some schools have only one teacher to a department, and some subjects are being taught at secondary level by non-specialists. Many witnesses told the Committee that staff morale was very low in both primary and secondary schools. These difficulties affect all the children in the area but Liverpool Blacks were even worse off than other young people in Liverpool 8. HMI investigated the number of Liverpool 8 students on certain courses in the Further Education colleges nearest to Toxteth. On two full-time catering courses and one hairdressing course, taking about 200 students altogether, teaching staff estimated that only three or four students were 'black'. The Race Relations Sub-Committee of the Liverpool Teachers' Association produced a pamphlet, some months before the disturbances of July 1981, saying it was: 'an undisputed fact … that black children in this city are under achieving in education'. What LEA provision there was related to ethnic minorities, the document claimed, was concentrated on the English language needs of recent immigrants.

HMI warned, in their Report, that further cuts in financial and other resources would damage staff morale and effectiveness, both of which were already under strain. They stressed, and our visits confirmed, that some teachers are 'resilient and resourceful', and working hard under difficult conditions, including unsuitable buildings and a general atmosphere of city decline, and alienation among many pupils and parents. They found that in one comprehensive school serving the area only 30 per cent of the intake had a reading age of ten or more on entry. Within this general picture of underachievement by 'black' and 'white' alike in the area, it was apparent from the written and oral evidence submitted to us that the Liverpool Black children were particularly low in attainment: partly because of the negative attitude towards them of some teachers, and, despite the dedication of other teachers, partly because of their own and their parents' sense of alienation, in a social structure that offers them no hope for the future.

Recently, some re organisation of secondary education has scattered some of the Liverpool Black children into new, mainly 'white' catchment areas, but not always with happy results. On one of our visits, a girl of 15 described to us how she had been the only 'Black' girl in a school and had not liked it because the others 'bossed her about'. When asked about this, she replied that she had had to go to hospital, once with a broken arm and once with a broken nose. She, and the other pupils present, found it unremarkable, and when the incident was later mentioned at a meeting of teachers and community workers they pointed out that Liverpool schools had always been like that for Liverpool Blacks. Those Liverpool Blacks who find employment are almost all in low-grade jobs, unlike other ethnic minority groups we have considered where there is generally more variety in the spectrum of employment. Expectations too are very low: to be a van-boy, a labourer, a shop assistant, clerical worker or machinist are ambitions; indeed to hope to get a job at all, of any sort, is 'flying high'. There are few who contemplate the possibility of higher education, and there is a realistic cynicism even about 'O' levels: 'You just lose time.' It is very rare indeed for a Liverpool Black youngster to proceed to University; two who had done so were named at meetings we attended. The University, sited in Liverpool 8, has some black students but not from the locality: they come from overseas or other parts of Britain. Its facilities are a constant reminder of the contrast between what locals can expect and what people from elsewhere receive.

Visiting Liverpool 8 and talking with witnesses there, the observer receives a very vivid impression of how strongly the situation of the Liverpool Black minority is affected by the special character of Merseyside itself. The established social and political structures perpetuate old practices and attitudes formed at different periods of history. The 'blacks' are simply left out of the pattern. For example, large firms, when they recruit new employees tend to advertise only within the firm enabling only relatives and friends of existing employees to apply. In cases where there are no 'black' employees already, racial inequality is thus perpetuated. A voluntary agency, South Liverpool Personnel, which tries to help young 'blacks' get jobs, said in evidence to us: 'Local employers claimed there was no discrimination – it was simply that no blacks were employed ... Liverpool was a commuter city: all the workers in the city centre travelled in from outlying white areas. Only 5 black people were employed on the buses and there were virtually no blacks in the city centre stores ... The council was a particularly bad employer.'

Liverpool Blacks do not only find it difficult to get work in the city centre: they risk insult or abuse in going there at all, and so their invisibility in the City's social life and power structure has become institutionalised. Until recent years; there was virtually no 'Black' involvement in any of the political parties locally.

Conclusion: Our consideration of the 'Liverpool Black' community highlights the important effect *local* factors can have on the experience and achievement of a particular ethnic minority community. It also illustrates how, despite concern having been expressed by a number of reports and committees over a period of ten years and more about the extreme degree of the problems facing this community, little real progress has yet been made to bring about the necessary changes in education and beyond. As the Home Affairs Committee concluded, in their 1981 Report: 'Racial disadvantage in Liverpool is in a sense the most disturbing case of racial disadvantage in the United Kingdom, because there can be no question of cultural problems or newness of language, and it offers a grim warning to all of Britain's cities that racial disadvantage cannot be expected to disappear by natural causes. The Liverpool Black Organisation warned the

Sub-Committee, 'what you see in Liverpool is a sign of things to come'. We echo that warning.

Educational Initiatives

The growing recognition, spurred on by the riots and informed by the Swann inquiry, that education was failing children in Liverpool 8, black children in particular, added momentum to initiatives to improve schooling and access to further and higher education. Most of these initiatives came from within Liverpool 8, from people and organisations who were well aware of educational problems and motivated to solve them. Wally Brown, then a youth worker who went on to head Liverpool Community College later in his career, describes some of the educational initiatives that he and others were involved in, particularly in the period around the riots of 1981.One of these was known as 'Elimu Wa Nane':

> I set up an education project in the Methodist Centre, which was called Elimu Wa Nane, 'education for eight' in Swahili. 'Education' is 'Elimu' and 'Wa Nane' was 'for eight': Education for Liverpool 8. And what my idea was, we had a youth club, we'd got kids getting bad deals at school. They go to college, and they get the Mickey Mouse courses, and you know ... they knew nothing about their black history. There had been a black history project at the youth centre. They had got some money for black history at the youth centre prior to that, but they had never got it running. So, they had all these books ... but it did not run. So, when I came back after university I worked as a community education worker and I set up a [small] room in the youth club. I said 'that was my room'. I made it into a library, with all black literature and the kids could come in. It was a quiet space. They could come in, they could read ... and there would be black magazines, there would be *Ebony* ... all the stuff.

I used to also, as part of my job, liaise with kids who were having trouble at school, maybe suspended. I got staff from the college to come in to do the teaching ... It was like a small education project.

I always remember, there were these three girls ... they had come from school, finished school, they would come, hanging around ... messing about, up in the office, messing on the typewriter. I would say, 'Stop messing with that stuff. Go and learn to type'. They said 'OK. We want to learn to type!' I said 'All right!' So I got three typewriters [laughs], I got the old Pitman's books [laughs], and I said to them 'Right, no messing. You come in and you go through that'. So they used to come in on an afternoon after school, they would do it. One of those girls is now an international banker for one of the main banks. She lives and works in Jersey and her family is still in Liverpool 8 ... and I often see her brother, and I say 'How's Lucy [not her real name]?' He says 'Oh, she's all over the world. She goes all over the world.' She's an executive in this bank. Lucy Jones [not her real name]. I can see her now, her little skirt on [laughs] ... [And] it all started from the typewriter [laughs] ...

I remember another guy who used to come in, he used to borrow books. He'd done his degree here in Liverpool, as a mature student, Simon Drake [not his real name] ... and he stood for [the] Council as an Independent in Toxteth. He's left Liverpool now. But I always remember he had brought some books back, and there's all bloody pencil lines in the book. I said 'Hey Simon, look at the book!' He said 'Wally, listen', he said 'The brethren, they can't read'. He said, 'What I have to do ... I'm underlining.' He said 'I use these books when we sit in groups, in someone's house, and I'm underlining things.' He said 'A little bit of pencil in your book is not a problem if it helps people read.'

Wally explains that the concept behind this education centre was not simply to help children pass exams, or to support those with special needs.

> It was more of a sort of support for all kids, and focus on black [history] because in those days, there were no black history books ... so, it was letting the kids see blackness in a positive light.

Wally and others had also been involved in the initial stages of the Black Access Course that would eventually be run from the Octagon Centre. This was one initiative that offered those who had been failed by the education system a second chance as mature students to enter higher education.

This chapter began by acknowledging the children and young people involved in and affected by the riots, and then went on to examine the wider context of this, including multiple failures of the education system. Recognition of these problems, including an official Inquiry, paved the way for change, adding momentum to positive initiatives originating in Liverpool 8. Without overstating the success of these initiatives or the extent of challenges remaining, there may be glimmers of hope, and grounds to suggest that the riots have had some positive legacies.

5

Economic Problems and Solutions

The Rialto, a former cinema that was burned down during the riots, has since been rebuilt as part of a housing development (Figures 5.1, 5.2). But this prominent symbol of regeneration, which stands at the busy intersection of Princes Avenue and Upper Parliament Street in the heart of Liverpool 8, masks a more complex story, in which some of the issues raised by the riots of 1981 have been addressed successfully, others unsuccessfully, while still others have been swept under the carpet.

Though their stories revolve primarily around policing, many of those who were involved in the riots also explain that tensions were fuelled by a combination of deprivation and discrimination. A combination of absolute poverty and relative disadvantage was expressed through rioting, targeted not simply at society, but more specifically at symbols of the Establishment and privilege. 'David', then a 16-year-old resident of Liverpool 8, explains why the Racquets Club was attacked:

> I remember when the Racquets Club went up ... Even now that makes feel like 'wow' – a private club for Judges, and [it] was situated on Parliament Street, Toxteth, L8. These were the judges we the community knew were inherently racist ... You should have seen this club! It had fine art on the wall, polished brass, bar facilities, everything the taxpayers' money

could buy. It was just shocking to think that you had this kind of over the top decadence in the middle of a deprived community with its lack of social housing, jobs, you know, people struggling to get by, and here you had this group of so-called 'social elite', sitting in the heart of this community ... they needed only to look out the window of their social club to see the reasons why the people stood there before them. They say in life nothing is certain but I was certain that place was to go up in flames and so it did!

The tensions and divisions described here were addressed in detail by the media, reporting the riots, as discussed in Chapter 3. They were also the subject of high-profile research, undertaken in the 1970s, which had been presented to various Parliamentary Select Committees (on employment, policing and racial disadvantage). This research painted a picture of disadvantage and racial discrimination, which had particularly severe consequences for Liverpool-born black people, as Gideon Ben-Tovim explains:

As our research work developed we were aware of a widespread pattern of social exclusion facing the Liverpool-born black community. Through the Merseyside Area Profile Group (a network of Sociology Department lecturers, researchers, students and members of the local community that I helped establish), we collected evidence of systematic racial inequalities and produced a series of publications. Despite being the longest standing black community in Britain, there were very few black people working for the City Council – less than 1 per cent in our earliest study.

Through research commissioned by the National Commission for Racial Equality we found evidence of the almost total exclusion of black people from decent council housing property, and the systematic lack of access to social care facilities (e.g. day care centres, sheltered accommodation or meals on wheels). There were informal colour bars or no-go areas in many facilities and areas of the city, for example in pubs, clubs, youth facilities. There was certainly a degree of social segregation, with the black community being confined to specific neighbourhoods. There really was then quite a deep-seated social exclusion, with people being labelled as outsiders despite being 'scousers'. There were also connections in the minds of the police and authorities with the red light district that persisted for a while in a part of Liverpool 8, together with some official resistance to the pattern of black–white intermarriage that was part of the fabric of the community. This might sound stark and one-sided, but that was the sort of analysis that we were developing based on the evidence we were accumulating and publishing in accessible form.

Historian P. J. Waller, writing in the early 1980s, summarises the economic problems experienced by Liverpool 8 at the time.

The last set of unemployment figures published for Liverpool before the July riots showed 81,629 jobless people contesting 1,019 vacancies; and the city's careers offices listed only a dozen openings for thousands of school leavers. Gloom was deepening, not lifting. Certainly the original economic *raison d'être* of Liverpool, its port, is in inexorable decline, from a combination of causes internal and external to the city; and, if British membership of the European Economic Community is to be permanent, the expectations must be that Liverpool will suffer, compared with east-coast or Channel ports, from inherent locational disadvantages, as well as from knock-on effects from the de-industrialisation of the north-west generally. Recent forecasts, both official and independent, by the Merseyside County Council's planning department and by a Liverpool University lecturer, Tony Lane, differ only in their

estimates of the depth of the depression, which is symptom-
atic of inescapable, fundamental, and enduring structural
change in the region. The former reckoned at best 20,000,
at worst 80,000, jobs might be lost from Merseyside between
1981 and 1986; the latter that overall the unemployment level
on Merseyside might rise from 16 per cent in 1981 to 22 per
cent in 1985. The combination of a shrinking economic base
and an increasing debit on the social account is cause for
grave concern.

Media attention to these economic problems, discussed in
Chapter 3, resonated with the Conservative government's
response to the crisis, which was essentially to look for market
solutions to social problems. At the centre of this strategy was
Prime Minister Margaret Thatcher's decision to send Michael
Heseltine, a senior and high profile minister in her government,
to Liverpool, where he set up temporary office and remained
for three weeks. This strategy was not entirely unwelcome or
unsuccessful, though it has been criticised for deflecting attention from some of the issues raised by the riots, and for seeking
economic growth without addressing discrimination within the
economy, as this chapter explains.

The Minister for Merseyside and
the Merseyside Task Force

Michael Heseltine arrived in Liverpool on 21 July 1981, and threw
himself into the task of understanding and addressing the city's
social, economic and environmental problems. On 26 August,
he announced a package of measures for Liverpool including a
series of economic incentives. He followed up this agenda at the
Conservative Party Conference, using his speech on 15 October
to make a plea for Britain's inner cities. In this way, he used

his experience in Liverpool to establish and develop a broader agenda, concerned with inner cities across the country. The riots prompted Heseltine to spend a sustained period of time in Liverpool, though his interest in the city had begun earlier, when he decided that the city's social and economic problems were compounded by – and could be addressed through – its physical environment, which was plagued by a mixture of industrial decline, toxic waste and neglect. Heseltine's direct intervention in Merseyside was also prompted by political considerations. Creating a regional development authority for Merseyside, he found a way to bypass politicians and political structures, which he found difficult to negotiate. When they came, the riots provided the 'Minister for Merseyside' with grounds to redouble his efforts, which had already begun. These events, he pointed out, were 'among the very worst' in the country.[1] Heseltine responded by sidestepping if not necessarily dismissing questions about law and order. 'No Conservative Government,' he said, 'could fail to support the forces of law and order in the face of such a challenge.' Heseltine's focus was, instead, on environmental and economic problems and free-market solutions, backed up with a limited amount of public money. He set out this case in his memoirs:

> Predictably, the voices of the left sought explanations and alibis, forgetful in the newly found freedom of opposition of the role of extremists in undermining Jim Callaghan's government. It was perhaps not sufficiently emphasised at the time how limited were the numbers of people actually involved and how dramatic the impact caused by the magnification of the headlines. If there was a moment when Enoch Powell's dread forecast in his 'rivers of blood' speech might have assumed a hideous reality, this surely was it.[2]

But, he argued, this was not a 'mass uprising' but instead a limited affray, albeit one which reflected deep social and economic problems and tensions.

> Close to the city centre, a few hundred yards from the Mersey, lay this isolated community. It embraced many thousands of people, living either in rundown nineteenth-century terraced housing or post-war, low-quality council accommodation. In Toxteth, the boarded-up properties, the empty, derelict, rubbish-strewn sites and the pervading street-corner atmosphere of hopelessness were proof of the long-term decline of the wider city.[3]

> As the days passed, it became more and more clear to me that there were projects that should have, in the main, long since been undertaken and that now lay within my capability to launch. At the end of my two and a half weeks I called a press conference. I was able to list thirteen initiatives. They included a town-planning brief to restore the Anglican Cathedral precinct, a scheme for the provision of community workshops for small firms, a government grant of £1 million for sporting facilities (to be matched by private money), a management training scheme for young unemployed at two separate centres and – the one that caught the headlines – the establishment of a Tate Gallery of the North on the old Albert Dock site.[4]

Heseltine continues: 'a list of initiatives wasn't enough' – it was necessary to drive them forward, so he visited Liverpool weekly for the next two years, working with a local task force he helped establish.

Heseltine's personal memories and individual role in the process of formulating and implementing a government response to the problems experienced by people in Liverpool 8 and other inner cities can be set in the broader context of developing regional and urban policy initiatives. These are explained by Jon Murden in *Liverpool 800*, the epic history of the city edited by John Belchem. Murden explains that the central government's interventions in Merseyside mobilised structures that had been established before the riots took place, when it championed a 'strongly market-orientated and property-led approach to urban regeneration'. This was advanced through the 1980 Local Government, Planning and Land Act which provided powers to establish Urban Development Corporations (UDCs) for the purpose of area regeneration, reclamation of derelict property, encouraging industrial and commercial development and ensuring the provision of social facilities and housing. One of the attractions of this policy, for a government that did not feel it could work with some local authorities, and in particular the authority in Liverpool, was that these development agencies would bypass local authorities, taking decisions quickly and establishing a business culture in regeneration practices and projects. The Merseyside Development Corporation (MDC) was one of the first two UDCs, which were established on 25 March 1981, and this put Liverpool at the heart of the government's urban policy, effectively paving the way for its responses to the riots that followed shortly afterwards. The MDC was charged with redeveloping an area covering 350 hectares of former docks including Liverpool South Docks and parts of the Northern Docks, most of which had closed in 1972, subsequently filling up with contaminated silt while their historic buildings fell into disrepair. The MDC began work dredging silt and improving buildings, particularly the historic Albert Dock, in the hope that a restored environment would lure business and investment back to the city. So, when the riots took place in Liverpool 8, the MDC was ready to act, which it did by stepping up schemes, many of which had already been conceived, but which assumed new local and national significance, as Jon Murden explains:

Reverberations from Toxteth were felt strongly in Whitehall where the government, fearful of the threat to public order, picked up on the need to further tackle the scale of 'economic and social deprivation in the poorest city in Britain'. Numerous fact-finding missions by senior Ministers to the riot zone searched for a solution to the 'Liverpool problem'. Ultimately a new initiative was launched in October 1981, a special Minister for Merseyside, Michael Heseltine, supported by a new administrative unit, the Merseyside Task Force (MTF) supposed to devise innovative strategies and projects to turn round Liverpool's long-term problems and encourage private sector investment in the inner city. In this respect the MTF had a number of successes, most notably creating over 1,000 jobs through the re-development of 35 hectares of previously derelict railway sidings into the Wavertree Technology Park, but equally important was the impact it had upon the MDC. Despite its brave plans, the MDC initially struggled to attract inward private commercial investment due to the fragility of the local economy, political instability and the poor image of Liverpool. The MTF dramatically changed its fortunes by encouraging the adoption of a regeneration strategy based more on tourism, leisure, housing and tertiary employment. This change in strategy was confirmed in December 1981 when the MTF charged the MDC with organising an International Garden Festival in Liverpool as a 'test of the continental model as a vehicle for the investment of resources targeting inner-city development'.

In organising the Garden Festival Liverpool and the MDC achieved a near miracle. 100 hectares of severely polluted land in the Dingle area were reclaimed and turned into a magnificent collection of display gardens, complete with Water Park and Festival Hall, in less than two-and-a-half years. The phrase 'jobs not trees' was heard in Liverpool once plans for the festival were announced, but criticism waned as attendances grew and the festival became the most popular tourist attraction of 1984 with over 3.4 million visitors through the turnstiles:

Virtually all reviews lauded the successful co-ordination of the numerous professionals involved. That so heavily polluted and disturbed a site could be cleared in such a short time was remarkable. But to do so while simultaneously addressing the complexities associated with the preparation of a major exposition made this a doubly significant achievement.

Indeed, it is not without significance that the Landscape Institute's award for the 'Most Influential Landscape Scheme 1970–2002', was awarded to Liverpool Garden Festival, cited for the popular appeal it acquired and the way it generated a 'cultural impulse, something beyond a legacy landscape'. 1984 also saw the tourist potential of the area further demonstrated by the success of the Tall Ships Race, which attracted over 2 million visitors, and the Albert Dock renovation that after the opening of the Tate Gallery in May 1988, 'an important cultural development which could make a large contribution to the tourism potential of the area', was able to attract over 3 million visitors annually. Having almost stumbled upon a successful formula for regeneration the MDC was then able to make impressive progress, success that in its wake would see Liverpool City Council embrace tourism as an economic driver for the future. In the immediate term, by 1988 the restoration of the dock system was nearing completion. According to the Department of Environment report entitled *Strategic Planning For Merseyside*, published in 1988:

£140 million of public investment has helped reclaim 97 hectares for residential and commercial development and 48 hectares for recreation and open space; to refurbish 135,000 square metres for housing and commercial uses, including the historic Albert Dock restoration. The MDC has created 1,160 jobs since 1981 and 94% of its contracts have been let to firms in the Merseyside area.

Despite these achievements, the MDC and MTF had mixed results, and their strategies have also been criticised, as the next sections explain.

Mixed Results

Interviewed on the twentieth anniversary of the riots, Liberal Democrat council leader Mike Storey spoke of 'tremendous optimism' in Granby and Toxteth, pointing to 'huge investment in the area' with unemployment 'halved' and the establishment of a 'multicultural school' and a women's hospital.[5] But, not far from the new Rialto building, an apparent symbol of the 'new Liverpool 8', there are some less encouraging traces of the riots and the area's social and economic problems. Granby Street, another epicentre of the riots, is no longer busy with shoppers and many of its buildings are boarded up, awaiting demolition. Wally Brown, speaking on the twentieth anniversary of the riots, observed that Granby Street had only declined, and was in a 'worse state' than ever: 'In terms of the road as a social centre, it is virtually non-existent.'[6] Lodge Lane has also experienced years of decline, and regeneration schemes have done more to prepare for new investment – houses and buildings giving way to open areas of grass and vacant lots – than to deliver actual regeneration (Figure 5.2). Meanwhile, flagship regeneration projects including the Garden Festival have not always been followed through. Though some of the Festival site has been developed for housing, other parts are still waiting for tenants and investment, decades after they were released for development (Figure 5.3). Twenty years after the riots, Lady

Margaret Simey, whose work as chair of the Police Authority is discussed in Chapter 3, said that the Garden Festival and regeneration schemes were misconceived. As she pointed out, the festival site stood derelict – as much of it does today – and the housing demolition and rebuilding schemes 'destroy[ed] the Caribbean community, dispersing a very close-knit and strong community'.[7] Liverpool-born novelist Beryl Bainbridge asked, in characteristically succinct style, what could have laid Liverpool so low: 'the rioters only gutted the Rialto, the Racquets Club, part of a hospital and most of Lodge Lane: people should ask who knocked down the rest of it?'[8] In 2003, the *Guardian* newspaper called the Garden Festival site 'a decaying monument to another grand cultural project that was meant to bring economic regeneration in its wake' and 'a cautionary tale to show what happens when politicians fail to think beyond the brief shelf-life of an ambitious project'.[9] Like Lady Simey, Wally Brown is pessimistic about the fruits of regeneration. 'In real terms,' he told the BBC twenty years after the riots, 'the young people who were involved on the street, their equivalents today are no better off than their counterparts 20 years ago.'[10]

But what do ordinary people, including residents and former residents, think about this today? Has the investment in Liverpool 8 made life any better? On the 25th anniversary of the riots, a BBC web forum invited members of the public to have their say on the question of whether 'regeneration projects and massive cash injections' had succeeded in bringing about change in Liverpool since 1981. Here are some of the responses, which paint a mixed picture at best:[11]

> There are significant poverty issues in other parts of the city, and they have all been let down. However there is the economic infrastructure – just look at all the new build – and look how much of that money is going to sub-contractors

from outside the city. I personally feel like crying when I see the remains of what was a vibrant, self-supporting community to what it is now. By that I mean an area which has been systematically destroyed by poor local government decisions and robbed of a lot of its individual character.

The main problem is people just do not want to live in inner city Liverpool – it has always had a poor reputation and since the docks' decline very high unemployment. This affects areas both in the South End and North End, and has led to the shocking depopulation of Lodge Lane, Granby, Scotland Road etc. There is no longer the economic infrastructure to support regeneration in these areas.

I went to school in L8 during the riots and have lived in Falkner Square, Toxteth – L8 for the past 5 years. It's a beautiful cosmopolitan area where the houses are selling like hot cakes as the area is restored back to its original grandeur. Okay there's the odd scally around causing mischief but on the whole this area of Toxteth is on the up. I went down Granby Street the other week and I can see no improvement from 25 years ago. It is as if the area has been abandoned by the council. Of course in a sense it has been like all the other areas outside of the city centre, robbed of funding to pay for capital of culture in the city centre.[12]

More sustained and up-to-date answers to the question of what has changed in Liverpool 8, socially and economically, through interventions such as Heseltine's, are provided through the oral histories which we conducted in 2010. Mike Boyle, who grew up in Liverpool 8, explains:

Gone are many of the old streets and small terraced houses of both Lodge Lane and Granby Street, with many of those streets now making way for much needed modern redeveloped housing where the old four- and six-roomed houses once stood. Gone is the busy thoroughfare that once was Granby Street with its numerous general stores, ironmongers, and the local butchers etc. A small number of the shop buildings still stand and continue to provide a limited service to the area's residents, other shops stand derelict and boarded up, adding to a picture of urban decay. Today's Lodge Lane bears no resemblance to the Lodge Lane of the 1950s, 60s and early 70s.

[Lodge Lane is] still a main thoroughfare – the rundown nature of a large percentage of the shops resembles a picture more akin to that of New York's South Bronx. Although some urban regeneration has been carried out much of the area still provides a lasting picture of urban decay and social exclusion. For the area's residents the struggle goes on in a never-ending quest to overcome the rigours of poverty and social deprivation.

Michael Simon, who also spent his childhood in the Granby area (and still lives in Liverpool 8 today), reflects on the changes he has – and has not – seen over the years. He refers to the dispersal of Liverpool-born black people from Liverpool 8 to other parts of the city in recent years, and suggests that this is not necessarily a symptom of social mobility, and that it could be another cause of vulnerability.

There's still no jobs for these kids in this area. There's even less things to do than when I was younger. I'm pretty sure that the way communities are now dispersing over the area … eventually I think an incident's going to flare up somewhere else and then you're going to get people coming back, you're going to get the diverse black communities come back together again. I expect that – it's not being pessimistic – I just expect that to come because I just don't see anything improving.

'David', who was 16 when the riots took place, feels that too little has changed since then.

> No, nothing really changed. Nothing changed at all. It looks prettier. Built a hospital, even when the bit of regeneration that took place in the community, the community didn't benefit from it. It was all outside workers, or workers from the north or the south end of the city. But the actual community itself didn't get any part of it.

Gideon Ben-Tovim puts this kind of disappointment in context, explaining that government initiatives did produce some benefits, but that these did not filter through to the people who needed them most.

> One of the legacies of that period was the movement to a greater regeneration of Liverpool as a whole, so the work of the Merseyside Task Force set up after the riots by Michael Heseltine certainly had a wide civic impact for Liverpool. In one sense the renaissance of Liverpool began after the riots in the 1980s with the Liverpool Garden Festival, the development of the Albert Dock, the establishment of the Merseyside Development Corporation, and later City Challenge, all of which had an important city-wide impact. Thus an effect of the riots was to bring Liverpool to the attention of national politicians and to kick-start a long and overdue process of regeneration, culminating in the 2008 Capital of Culture achievement.

> But I don't think that such a huge amount was actually invested in Liverpool 8 after the riots, as compared to what was spent on the wider city. There was some cosmetic improvement to the Princes Avenue Boulevard. A process of housing improvement began, seeing in due course some of the removal of the worst quality council accommodation in Liverpool 8.

There were some modest targeted initiatives that emerged through the Task Force in that period that have had an impact in trying to achieve a better degree of black representation in certain fields of employment. Thus there was a positive action training scheme which involved the housing associations offering places and the Community College delivering the training, leading to the eventual employment of some black housing staff. This had some impact on the local housing associations, and helped some individuals to develop themselves in that field.

The significant investment of the NHS in the Women's Hospital in Liverpool 8 can be seen as a positive outcome of the riots, a deliberate attempt by the then Dean of Liverpool to invest in Liverpool 8 through his 'Project Rosemary'.

So in the period since the riots we have seen some investment in housing and the urban infrastructure; some incremental bits of positive action training, including housing associations and social work; the College/University Access partnership and the sustained College recruitment of Liverpool 8 students; a successful new primary school/children's centre; a major NHS investment in the area; some improvements in the workforce profiles of the City Council and the NHS.

However, overall I would say there have not been enough targeted interventions, and a lot of what we saw after the riots was a rather general regeneration which on the whole bypassed Liverpool 8. Within Liverpool 8 itself some of the worst council accommodation has been cleared and better council or social housing accommodation put in its place, but even here there are the 'Three Streets' in Granby that have still not had their future decided, and Granby Street itself has not been regenerated, with many boarded-up shops remaining. However, this is bordered by a new school and attached Sure Start Centre (of which I am Chair of Governors), which

received a recent 'Outstanding' Ofsted inspection assessment for the school. So if you look in the Liverpool 8 area,
the facelift and investment have been uneven. Princess Park,
the main local park, has only just recently had some improvement, though the small park in Falkner Square was transformed relatively soon after the riots.

Criticisms of the Environmental/Economic Strategy

Environmental and economic responses to the riots were criticised for deflecting attention away from the thorniest issues
they had raised: policing and racism. As Michael LeRoy put
it in his Evangelical Coalition report, 'Heseltine changed the
agenda. While local people lifted the police issue for all to see
Michael Heseltine raised the environmental issues even higher,
obscuring all else, and attracting a new band-wagon to other
issues that needed action'.[13] Lady Simey dismissed the economic
agenda as a distraction, arguing that '[it] is not the unemployment people resent – Liverpool's has always been higher. It's
that if you happen also to have a black face, there is no escape
from the poverty.'[14] This echoed the local MP's comments, at
the time of the riots, that the unrest was not about unemployment and economic distress, but rather discrimination and
inequality within this more generally disadvantaged context.
As he put it:

> I do not believe that unemployment was the cause of the
> trouble, nor is it correct to blame it on the housing in that
> area. The area of the rioting has many thousands of new
> houses. I believe that these events came about because,
> rightly or wrongly, there is a genuine belief not only in the
> black community but in the white community that in that
> area the enforcement of law and order is not even-handed.[15]

What was needed, according to the Member for Toxteth, was not money but 'trust and confidence between the police and the community'. Similar points were made by the Catholic Archbishop and the Anglican Bishop, Derek Worlock and David Sheppard, who acknowledged the extent of economic distress in Liverpool but dismissed suggestions that the riots were essentially the 'grievances of unemployed youngsters' or frustration with 'abysmally poor housing, disillusion with local government, and despair'. These issues were also present, they agreed, but the bishops detected something more profound in the riots: a desire to be acknowledged and listened to: 'Certainly the people on the spot had little hope of ever having a real say about their future. Asked what they wanted, they would reply more often that they wanted to be listened to, than that they wanted any specific reforms.'[16]

Thus, while interventions by the MDC and MTF were criticised for their mixed results – delivering growth in some areas and not in others, and offering limited value for money – it was also felt that they failed to tackle directly the issues of racism and discrimination which the riots had brought to the surface. These issues could have been more effectively brought within the economic agenda had the authorities paid more attention to the ways in which growth and investment might benefit different sections of society, rather than simply focussing on overall levels of growth. As Jon Murden points out, the government spent £170 million of public money to attract just £25 million in private investment, creating no more than 1,500 jobs 'and apparently doing very little to help the deprived communities of the inner city'. Murden expands upon this last point, noting that, though it 'had initially emphasised its intention to take account of the needs of ethnic minorities in Liverpool', the MTF 'launched only a few projects to benefit the black community' and these were treated as 'secondary to broader Merseyside-wide initiatives that were almost entirely irrelevant to the black population'. Murden concludes that '[the] work of the MDC was slow to bear fruit, however, and had little impact upon the seemingly ever-growing numbers of long-term unemployed. Furthermore, the social costs of unemployment proved to be far from evenly spread across Liverpool'.[17]

The economic inequalities within Liverpool, and specifically between racial and ethnic communities within the city, were addressed in a House of Commons Select Committee enquiry in 1986. Evidence submitted to this Committee, on the occasion of its visit to Liverpool on 10 February of that year, provides detailed assessments of discrimination that persisted within the city five years after the riots. The evidence, compiled by the Merseyside Community Relations Council, Liverpool Black Caucus and Merseyside Area Profile Group, was published 'in order to give the widest possible airing' to the issues it raised, concerned with 'racial discrimination and disadvantage in employment facing black people in Liverpool'. The report 'stresses the continuing failure of central and of local government, and local employers and financial institutions, to take the steps necessary to improve the situation'.[18]

> The initial and major point we must make to the Committee is the continually devastating problem of massive unemployment facing the black community in Liverpool. This is a longstanding problem in this city, and we must stress that central and local government responses to this issue have been shamefully inadequate and irresponsible. The Committee must, in our view, leave Liverpool determined to bring about real change, both nationally and locally, to this drastic situation which is clearly one of the factors, along with problems related to policing practices, underlying the social tensions and disorders that have been experienced in the city.

What is required, then, is a major, concerted effort by central and local government, public and private sector, to work with local black and ethnic minority organisations to transform the employment profile and the general economic base of the black community in Liverpool. As a result of generations of direct and indirect racial discrimination, and associated racial disadvantage, there has been a constant process of deskilling of the local community which now requires targeted intervention in a range of sectors: this includes opening up local employment opportunities, providing more training for skilled and professional career development, furnishing support for small business and co-operative enterprises, and finally providing a larger framework for the development of a more flourishing local economy.

In this respect, we regret to say that despite the adoption of an Equal Opportunity Statement in early 1981, there has been very little progress in the practical implementation of this policy, and indeed over the last fifteen months there has been a total regression as a result of the decision of the Labour leadership on the Council to appoint on purely sectarian political grounds a completely inexperienced, unqualified and totally unacceptable candidate to the post of Principal Race Adviser, and also to abolish the Race Relations Liaison Committee.

We would therefore ask the Select Committee to use their influence to press the Council to take up the range of practical measures and initiatives suggested to them over the last five years with respect to developing employment and training opportunities, changing and monitoring general recruitment practices and procedures, influencing local contractors, initiating and supporting positive action and specialist schemes, [including filling vacant section 11 posts] and supporting black community groups and small businesses.

We would ask the Select Committee, again, to use their influence to really push local private sector employers and the financial institutions to take a much more interventionist stance to promote positive action measures that will make a substantial difference to the opportunities and prospects facing the local black community.

Central Government has to adapt a much more interventionist stance in a number of ways:
- in its own role as an employer
- in its role as supplier of contracts with other employers
- in its influence over local authority employment practices
- in its use of anti-discrimination legislation
- in its inner city policies
- in its relationship with government bodies such as Manpower Services Commission

The city has over the past five years in particular seen flying visits from party leaders, politicians, and many other delegations. Ministers have been given responsibility for Merseyside, yet there has been little visible change in terms of black employment opportunities. Meanwhile current irresponsible confrontation by the City Council with the black community is allowed to continue and along with this, there persists the total dogmatic in-action by the Council on proven massive racial inequalities.

For Gideon Ben-Tovim, then, much of the 'moderate political progress [formerly achieved] was dismantled from 1983–7 ... when an aggressively "colour-blind" Militant group controlled the Labour City Council'.

The economic agenda, defined in the wake of the riots, could not ignore the issues of race, ethnicity and discrimination, which the riots had raised. As Margaret Simey observed, there was an urgent need to address discrimination within economic activities, in both the public and private sectors. In 1981, she pointed out that the Liverpool police force had contained only four black policemen out of 5,000, while the Liverpool Corporation had a scarcely superior record, with 31 black teenagers and 169 adults among 30,000 employees.[19] This echoed arguments, put to Scarman when he visited the city on 16 October 1981, that the riots reflected deprivation. Like policing, deprivation was experienced differently by different ethnic and racial communities, with Liverpool-born black people suffering the worst:[20]

> In the course of the discussion with the Police Committee the importance of social conditions, especially unemployment, as a factor in the background to the disorders had been mentioned. The vitiating effect of unemployment was again mentioned when Lord Scarman met the Leader of Liverpool City Council, Sir Trevor Jones, and the Leader of the Labour, and Deputy Leader of the Conservative Groups on the Council, together with its Chief Executive and Community Relations Officer. The Council representatives pointed out that very substantial local authority resources had been spent in Liverpool 8 over the years: it would not therefore be correct, in their view, to describe the area as substantially more deprived than certain other parts of Liverpool. Nor had the disorders been racial: both black and white youths had been involved. Rather, they had been a revolt against authority, particularly the police, fuelled by the central problem of unemployment. Sir Trevor Jones described the steps which the City Council was taking to ensure that a proper proportion of members of ethnic minority communities were recruited to its work-force, and to an exercise the Council had conducted to consult local opinion by means of a questionnaire: the answers to large-scale unemployment, however, lay in central government's hands.

This evidence called not simply for absolute growth and economic recovery, but for targeted and socially just investment, which would include Liverpool's black community and other marginalised residents of Liverpool 8.

Scarman's conclusions and reflections resonate with much that was being said locally, by people who understood deprivation and discrimination first hand, and looked not simply for economic growth and regeneration, but for socially just, targeted forms of investment. Looking back over the past 30 years, Wally Brown reflects that the economic stimulus measures have been poorly targeted both geographically and socially.

> I couldn't understand if you got a riot in Toxteth, or a riot in Liverpool 8, why do you have a Minister for Merseyside? Merseyside goes as far as St Helens. St Helens is ten miles away. What's the relevance between that and creating jobs in St Helens? It's not going to bloody help Toxteth! It's got to be a much more local focus and so in a sense, for me, that was a non-starter. It enabled them to put initiatives in Merseyside, and say 'we've put this in, and that in' which bore no reflection to anything in Toxteth ... but they could say they did things, because it would be easier to do things in a wider context ... because they knew they could not, they would not, they were not going to be able to do anything in there [Liverpool 8]. That's my cynical view of it.

> Now, the things that came afterwards were the Hospital, the Garden [Festival] Centre, the Albert Dock. People say the Albert Dock's a fantastic thing but it did nothing to help Toxteth. There was nothing for Toxteth, and the Garden [Festival] Centre which was derelict not long after. There are plans to redevelop it now, but you know 30 years later! So, that didn't give anything to Liverpool ... all that waterfront up there was developed, but again, it didn't give anything to Toxteth.

I went round with Heseltine a few years ago, and he was shown these houses. Even the houses they built, they destroyed the community that was there. I was involved in some regeneration studies there in Liverpool, and one of the experts on regeneration was saying 'So, the houses on the streets there, the grid pattern of those streets should have been retained.' But instead they knocked them down and built cul-de-sacs, and put these cardboard houses up. So yes, they put some houses there, but the key thing was the infrastructure has not been addressed. There are no shops. There's no quality of life for people in terms of the infrastructure and, Lodge Lane is slowly beginning to come back with a few shops here and there, a few, you know ... mainly community based things. But again Lodge Lane was quite a decent thriving sort of shopping area. It's slowly coming back.

Unemployment in Toxteth is 50%. Unemployment in that area is 50% amongst young people. So, they are no better ... the jobs are not there. The economic situation is no better. You still don't see many black faces when you go into the town. As I've said to you before, I go into the town centre in Liverpool and look for the black faces. You don't find many. Why is it that if I go to Manchester, I can see ... all over Manchester city centre, even the prestigious areas, [like] St Anne's Square and all those places, there are black people working there. There are black people managing shops. So, nothing has changed in that respect.

Wally's sense that the riots have left an economic legacy, but that this has been poorly targeted, mirrors to a degree the assessment put forward by Chief Constable Jon Murphy (below), who has known Liverpool 8 since he worked there as a police constable, thirty years ago. Though he feels optimistic about changes within policing – he feels that 'police are far better engaged with communities than they have ever been at any time in their history' and notes that there are now 'plenty of local black police officers and black support staff', including black police in the 'senior ranks' – Murphy finds that black people are still disadvantaged and excluded, economically and socially.

> What you can't get away from is still today, sadly ... black people are still disproportionately disadvantaged, and the point they're starting from, even with the positive action work that we do to try and encourage people to come in, there is still lots of young black people who really have got very little chance of getting into the police, simply because of their starting point. We have made lots of progress, but we'd like it to be better.

Notes

1 Michael Heseltine, *Life in the Jungle: My Autobiography* (London: Hodder & Stoughton, 2000), p. 215.
2 Heseltine, *Life in the Jungle*, p. 215.
3 Heseltine, *Life in the Jungle*, p. 218.
4 Heseltine, *Life in the Jungle*, p. 225.
5 Rohrer Finlo, 'Toxteth's Long Road to Recovery', *BBC News Online* Thursday, 5 July 2001, http://news.bbc.co.uk/1/hi/uk/1416198.stm.
6 Finlo, 'Toxteth's Long Road to Recovery'.
7 Finlo, 'Toxteth's Long Road to Recovery'.
8 Beryl Bainbridge, 'The Lullaby Sound of Houses Falling Down', *Sunday Times*, 19 July 1981.
9 'History Lesson for Future Capital of Culture', *Guardian*, 24 November 2003. See Jon Murden, 'City of Change and Challenge: Liverpool Since 1945', in John Belchem (ed.), *Liverpool 800: Culture, Character, History* (Liverpool: Liverpool University Press, 2006), pp. 393–485.
10 Finlo, 'Toxteth's Long Road to Recovery'.
11 http://www.bbc.co.uk/liverpool/content/articles/2006/06/28/toxteth_anniversary_feature.shtm.
12 http://www.bbc.co.uk/liverpool/content/articles/2006/06/28/toxteth_anniversary_feature.shtm.
13 LeRoy, *Riots in Liverpool 8*, p. 46.
14 Finlo, 'Toxteth's Long Road to Recovery'.
15 *Hansard* House of Commons 1981: Mr Richard Crawshaw (Liverpool, Toxteth), 6 July.

16 Worlock and Sheppard, *A Time for Healing*, pp. 167–68.

17 Murden, 'City of Change and Challenge', p. 439.

18 Merseyside Community Relations Council, Liverpool Black Caucus and Merseyside Area Profile Group, 1985, Evidence submitted to the House of Commons Select Committee on Employment on the occasion of their visit to Liverpool on February 10th 1986.

19 P. J. Waller, 'The Riots in Toxteth, Liverpool: A Survey', *New Community* 9.3 (1981–82).

20 *Scarman Inquiry Report*, p. 152.

Conclusion
Looking Back and Moving On

S ome people suggest that it is now time to move on, and stop harping on about riots that took place thirty years ago. They point out that Liverpool has seen worse riots – members of minority communities were hounded out of their houses and even killed by an angry mob in 1919 – and they have been dwarfed by uprisings, bloodshed and wars in the last three decades. We have found, though, that people do still remember the riots of 1981, and this book has illustrated some of the reasons why. By remembering the riots, and the reasons for them, the people of Liverpool and further afield have faced up to some difficult issues: racism and racial discrimination in government, policing and education; the problems of inner cities and divided communities; the failure of a market economy to deliver a fair deal to all members of society; and, most importantly, questions about how to address and even solve these challenges.

Each chapter in this book has identified both problems and solutions, also asking what has been solved and what remains to be addressed. In each case, different people have come to different conclusions about how far we have come since 1981. While all this has been taking place, Liverpool has changed, and Liverpool 8 has changed with it. The area is no longer as strongly identified with Liverpool-born black people, as those communities have dispersed, and have been replaced to some extent by first- and second-generation immigrants from other parts of the world, and by people who identify along religious rather than racial or ethnic lines, notably as Muslims. Diversity and multicultural community are nothing new to Liverpool 8, as this book has shown, but their forms have changed over time, as Figure 6.1 illustrates, in a view of Granby which points to the coexistence of Christians and Muslims in an area that has found modest forms of economic and social renewal.

Perhaps the most striking change in Liverpool 8 since 1981 has been a dispersal of the Liverpool-born black community and an influx of black and minority ethnic groups. Paul Adams, who grew up in Liverpool 8, reflects:

> I think one of the things that has changed is there's much less clear identity in Liverpool 8 community or Granby commu-nity, it's much more spread out obviously, many more black people now live down Smithdown Road, Kensington and that's mainly through migrant workers coming in. It's become much more diverse.

Jon Murphy, the Chief Constable, also notes the changing profile of Liverpool 8, which roughly corresponds to a police district known as E4. There, he says, 'there's something like 37 or 38 different languages spoken', and some older residents do not speak English, and rely on their children, who learn to speak English in schools, for their communication with the police and other authorities.

Michael Simon, who was 13 at the time of the riots and has continued to live in the area, suggests that the new arrivals have helped to bring about a sense of renewal, if not recovery:

> I kind of like the idea of the latest wave of immigration that we've had, which everyone has an opinion on. For me if you

look at Lodge Lane now, it's totally organic, rebuilt itself from
basically the white flight that happened after the riots and
actually when I was working for a community organisation,
we went round filming, trying to collect stories about the
shops that went there and [there were] some amazing stories.

The dispersal of Liverpool-born black people has been accompanied by the decline of some community organisations, while
the arrival of immigrants has resulted in the emergence of new
groups. Gideon Ben-Tovim:

With respect to community infrastructure some of the older
community centres, for example Charles Wootton and the
Liverpool 8 Law Centre have gone. Those were both quite
dependent on City Council funding, and ultimately came up
against decisions linked to value for money. The closures of
both the Charles Wootton and the Liverpool 8 Law Centre
went without a great deal of community opposition and
noise, although they both provided significant services in
their time and were important community institutions.

But new centres have come into prominence instead. Kuumba
Imani is an important centre at the top of Princes Rd. This
is a women-led organisation and a community resource that
also provides the Leadership of Merseyside Black History
Month. This centre is supported by other organisations,
including the Primary Care Trust (that I chair): we house
a number of our staff in there, to be close to the community, to support the centre and to seek to ensure the PCT
is actively promoting racial equality in the NHS. Crawford
House opened further down the road after many years of
campaigning, another newer building in the community
with a small-business focus. And there are newer organisations in the community as well such as the Al-Ghazali Centre
in Earle Road, whilst the Mosque is very busy and expanding

its premises and activities. So there is an evolution of newer infrastructure developments as well as some that have been closed, showing that there are still many vibrant organisations in a very changing Liverpool 8.

Much of this book has been about policing, and relationships between police and communities, which the riots exposed. Memories of resentment towards the police ran vividly through the oral histories we collected for this book. Evidence collected in the 1990s on policing in Merseyside, and the belated acknowledgement of institutional racism in the Macpherson Report (1999), show that problems remained with policing, both locally and nationally, for decades after the Liverpool riots. The government's official response, which concentrated in the short and medium term on social and economic problems, postponed rather than circumvented the need for thoroughgoing reforms of policing, facing up to and rooting out racism. It would be naive to think that process is complete, and it would be unrealistic to seek a consensus on this subject, since different people will continue to have different views and to speak from different experiences. However, Chief Constable Jon Murphy's optimistic assessment – that Merseyside police have 'really good community relations' in an environment that is 'interestingly far more multi-cultural than it was then' – is less controversial than it might have been several years ago.

Feelings on economic change are equally mixed. As discussed in Chapter 5, many people felt that the government's economically driven response to the riots, revolving around the Minister for Merseyside's high-level visit to the city in 1981, was simply divisive, bringing some growth but not tackling old divisions. Derek Murray, who worked at the Caribbean Centre, reflects:

You ... got a situation where a certain amount of money came in and was released for regeneration activities in Liverpool 8. But in a lot of ways that has proved very divisive. So, if you just take the thing with Heseltine, for example, the Garden Festival site. Now, the Garden Festival site is right at the bottom of my road, where I live in Liverpool 17, and how many years are we now, we're pushing on for 30 years, [and] it's still a very touchy subject, and if you think back, this was the immediate response. I know the plans were already in hand, but the immediate response was, let's release some money, let's do the Garden Festival site, yeah ... and this was meant to be a response to the socio-economic decline of Toxteth and Liverpool 8, because this was actually, technically, within that area.

[But] the way that was executed, I think has continued ... that kind of idea, or that kind of sense of exclusion [has] in a lot of ways [continued] and I think that cut quite deeply for a lot of people, because there was a lot of money spent there. There was a lot of work that went on, and as we all know basically, the work didn't go to people in Liverpool 8, and in fact, people in Liverpool 8 ... the sort of activities that were put on there, were not things that were designed to appeal to people in Liverpool 8 ... and people in Liverpool 8, many couldn't afford to go there.

Claire Dove, who also refers to the demise of community organisations in Liverpool 8, looks back over the changes that have variously been witnessed and driven by people in the area, pointing to some positive changes but stressing that 'the only initiatives that came out of the riots that did impact on our community were those set up by members of the black community'. She expands upon and explains this point:

After the riots the government tried some initiatives to help with unemployment and regeneration. Michael Heseltine came to Liverpool and became minister for Merseyside, and one of his major initiatives was the Garden Festival and he also engineered the transformation of Parliament Street with trees and grass verges and eventually under Project Rosemary the Women's Hospital was built. But what annoyed me, and what made me extremely angry was that black people didn't work on anything. It did not bring employment or change the root causes of why the riots had taken place. It was purely a cosmetic venture and apart from the hospital which local women would use as patients, none of these initiatives impacted on the lives of us in our community.

The only initiatives that came out of the riots that did impact on our community were those set up by members of the black community. The Charles Wootton Technology Centre, L8 Defence Committee, Liverpool 8 Law Centre and the Black Women's Group; all these were there to serve and support our community

After the riots there were marches against the brutality of the police, especially against the racist viewpoints of the Chief Constable Ken Oxford, who was the most sinister and racist man you could ever have in charge of the police. It was a coming together of trade unions, of communities all over that could see what happened to that black community and wanted to stand in support. Post-riots however different tactics by the community were used ... we tackled unemployment ... to give better life chances to our children in schools, but we knew the biggest battle was to fight the institutionalised racism within society ... but there was no turning back.

But my concern now, ... 30 years since the riots, is that we did grow a mini infrastructure within the community to support and offer opportunities. We did see some of our children achieving and young people going to university, there were employment opportunities and it was great to see some members of our communities employed by the local council. We did grow a number of key organisations to support our community, but unfortunately many are now gone, Liverpool 8 Law Centre, Charles Wootton College and Technology Centre, all gone, and with the current economic climate more will [go]. We are still a long way off having true equality.

Others, however, present a more optimistic account of some of the changes that have taken place, not least the European Capital of Culture festival, which took place in 2008. 'Nick', who was 18 when the riots happened, finds some hope in the Capital of Culture and the decade of New Labour government.

Through my life, I've witnessed no money in the city, and no development. And now all this development, because of the Capital of Culture, but also because it's been a different government party for the last twelve years. And it's quite funny to see the city changing. Suddenly get a bit of investment and change and all that and it's really good ... I think the 08 thing is really good and positive.

It's been brilliant watching it change and especially the amount of work in the last few years, you know. The Albert Dock and all that, and I think we're slightly different than other cities. We've got a lot more to offer and people don't really see that, you know. I think, just how many comedians, how many bands come from here, the football teams ... the theatre here, how strong it is, all the arts and all that. I think as arts and media and all that ... it's natural in this city ... naturally funny people, naturally talented people, naturally good bands. That's why we get not just the Beatles, but since then, and before then there's been bands.

So, I think, really, I think that's what makes this city if I'm honest, is the people. Just different walks of life, I just think, we're all just scousers aren't we. We like the lark ... humour about things, and I don't think we like to take ourselves too seriously. That's why I think I could never live anywhere else to be honest. The clubs, the pubs, everything. The people are just nosey. They're interested in your life. That's the way we are.

I think we've had the odds stacked against us for so long. Not just the last twelve years, or the twelve years before that, but even before that. Imagine this city years ago when there used to be all these different nationalities coming in from the docks. All the different people that have come from all over the world ...

So, in economic change, as in other spheres, it is possible to find a range of views, including some who feel sure that nothing fundamental has been resolved since 1981, and others who feel more optimistic.

Martin Luther King once declared that '[riots] are the voices of the unheard'. Was he right, in relation to Liverpool? The evidence and memories presented in this book suggest that he was. Some rioters, particularly those who came into the city from outside after the first night of rioting, seem to have had their own agendas and interests. Others, though, were residents of Liverpool 8, angered and wronged by the police, and alienated by years of deprivation and discrimination. For them, rioting was a way of being heard. For Michael Simon, this was therefore a 'legitimate protest'. He explains that remembering it has been and can continue to be important for people in Liverpool 8 – looking back and moving on:

This was a legitimate protest as far as I'm concerned ... You grew up with the sense of life that 'As soon as I grow up, I

want to get out of here', which I did as well, but then I think
I kind of turned myself around and for me that was like the
beginning of change, by saying 'Hang on, let me understand
what's gone on in the past and try and understand why I'm
here and why this is so ... '

Sources and Further Reading

Note on Sources

Some of the material quoted here, particularly that from academic sources, originally included extensive footnotes. It would not have been practical or appropriate to include these in full in this book, so they have mostly been left out. It is of course possible to find these by consulting the original texts.

Sources

Archbishop of Canterbury's Commission on Urban Priority Areas, *Faith in the City: A Call for Action by Church and Nation*, The Report of the Archbishop of Canterbury's Commission on Urban Priority Areas (London: Church House Publishing, 1985).

Archbishop of Canterbury's Commission on Urban Priority Areas, *Faith in the City: A Call for Action by Church and Nation, The Popular Version* (London: Christian Action, 1985).

Ben-Tovim, Gideon, Viv Brown, Dave Clay, Ian Law, Linda Loy and Protasia Torkington (eds.), *Racial Disadvantage in Liverpool – An Area Profile*. Evidence submitted to the Parliamentary Home Affairs Committee Session 1979–1980 on Racial Disadvantage (Liverpool: Merseyside Area Profile Group, 1980).

Benyon, John (ed.), *Scarman and After: Essays Reflecting on Lord Scarman's Report, the Riots and their Aftermath* (Oxford: Pergamon, 1984).

Bunyan, Tony, 'The Police against the People', *Race and Class* 23.2/3 (1981), pp. 153–70.

Burgess, Jacquelin A., 'News from Nowhere: The Press, the Riots and the Myth of the Inner City', in Jacquelin Burgess and John R. Gold (eds.), *Geography, the Media and Popular Culture* (London: Croom Helm, 1985), pp. 192–228.

CARF (Campaign Against Racism and Fascism) Collective, 'The Riots', *Race and Class* 23.2/3 (1981), pp. 223–50.

Cornelius, John, *Liverpool 8*, illustrated by the author (London: John Murray, 1982).

Gifford, A.M., Wally Brown and Ruth Bundey, *Loosen the Shackles: First Report of the Liverpool 8 Inquiry into Race Relations in Liverpool* (London: Karia Press, 1989).

Heseltine, Michael, *Life in the Jungle: My Autobiography* (London: Hodder & Stoughton, 2000).

Johnson, Linton Kwesi, 'Mekkin Histri', http://www.lintonkwesijohnson.com.

LeRoy, Michael G., *Riots in Liverpool 8: Some Christian Responses* (research report commissioned, printed and distributed by the Evangelical Coalition for Urban Mission, London, 1983).

Liverpool Black Caucus, *The Racial Politics of Militant in Liverpool: The Black Community's Struggle for Participation in Local Politics 1980–1986* (ed. G. Ben-Tovim) (Liverpool: Merseyside Area Profile Group/London: The Runnymede Trust, 1986).

Liverpool 8 Defence Committee, 'Why Oxford Must Go', in CARF (Campaign Against Racism and Fascism) Collective, 'The Riots', *Race and Class* 23.2/3 (1981), pp. 230–31.

Liverpool 8 Law Centre, 'Response to Merseyside Police Statement', in *Racism in the Force* (Liverpool: Liverpool 8

Law Centre, 1998).

Merseyside Community Relations Council, *Liverpool Black Caucus and Merseyside Area Profile Group*, Evidence submitted to the House of Commons Select Committee on Employment on the occasion of their visit to Liverpool on February 10th, 1986.

Merseyside Community Relations Council, *Senior Community Relations Officer's Report*, 11th Annual Report, 17 September 1981.

Morris, Rachel, 'A Summary of The Stephen Lawrence Inquiry' (Cm 4262-l), Report of an Inquiry by Sir William Macpherson of Cluny, Presented to Parliament by the Home Secretary, February 1999, http://www.law.cf.ac.uk/tlru/Lawrence.pdf (last accessed 29 November 2010).

Murden, Jon, 'City of Change and Challenge: Liverpool Since 1945', in John Belchem (ed.), *Liverpool 800: Culture, Character, History* (Liverpool: Liverpool University Press, 2006).

Nelson, W. *Black Atlantic Politics: Dilemmas of Political Empowerment in Boston and Liverpool* (New York: State University of New York Press, 2000).

O'Brien, David, 'Who Pays the Piper? Understanding the Experience of Organisations Sponsoring the Liverpool European Capital of Culture', report, October 2008, edited by Impacts 08; http://www.liv.ac.uk/impacts08/Papers/Impacts08(Oct08) WhoPaysThePiper-SponsorReport.pdf.

Scarman, George Leslie, Baron, *The Brixton Disorders 10–12 April 1981: Report of an Inquiry by Lord Scarman*, Cmnd. 8427 (London: HMSO, 1981).

Scarman, George Leslie, Baron, 'An Epilogue' (dated 25 May 1983), in John Benyon (ed.), *Scarman and After: Essays Reflecting on Lord Scarman's Report, the Riots and their Aftermath* (Oxford: Pergamon, 1984), pp. 259–61.

Simey Papers: Liverpool University Special Collections D396/54 (5 boxes).

Swann, Lord (Chairman), *Education for All: The Report of the Committee of Enquiry into the Education of Children from Ethnic Minority Groups*, Presented to Parliament by Lord Swann, Cmnd 9453 (London: HMSO, 1985).

Swann, Michael, *Education for All: A Brief Guide* (London: HMSO, 1985).

Waller, P. J., 'The Riots in Toxteth, Liverpool: A Survey', *New Community* 9.3 (1981–82).

Whyte, D., 'Contextualising Police Racism: The Aftermath of the Macpherson Report and the Local Response on Merseyside' (unpublished, Liverpool John Moores University, 2002).

Worlock, Derek, and David Sheppard, *A Time for Healing* (London: Hodder & Stoughton, 1988; Harmondsworth: Penguin, 1989).

Young, Martin, *BBC Listener Magazine*, 2 November 1978, http://www.diversemag.co.uk, accessed November 2010.

Additional Sources and Reading

Bishops' Advisory Group on Urban Priority Areas, *Staying in the City: Faith in the City Ten Years On* (London: Church House, 1995).

Ben-Tovim, Gideon, John Gabriel, Ian Law and Kathleen Stredder, *The Local Politics of Race* (Basingstoke: Macmillan, 1986).

Benyon, J., and J. Solomos (eds.),*The Roots of Urban Unrest* (Oxford: Pergamon, 1987).

Brown, Jacqueline Nassy, *Dropping Anchor, Setting Sail: Geographies of Race in Black Liverpool* (Princeton, NJ: Princeton University Press, 2005).

Cashmore, E. E., and E. McLoughlin (eds.), *Out of Order? Policing Black People* (London: Routledge, 1991).

Cross, M., and M. Keith (eds.), *Racism, the City and the State* (London: Routledge, 1993).

Clutterbuck, R., *The Media and Political Violence* (Basingstoke: Macmillan, 1993).

Dawson, J., and M. Parkinson, 'Merseyside Development Corporation, 1981–1989', in M. Keith and A. Rogers (eds.), *Hollow Promises? Rhetoric and Reality in the Inner City* (London: Mansell, 1991).

Field, S., and P. Southgate, *Public Disorder* (London: HMSO, 1982).

Gordon, P., 'The Police and Racist Violence in Britain', in T. Bjorgo and R Witte (eds.), *Racist Violence in Europe* (Basingstoke: Macmillan, 1993).

Hall, S., 'The Lessons of Lord Scarman', *Critical Social Policy*, 2.2 (1982), pp. 66–72.

Holdaway, S., *The Racialisation of British Policing* (Basingstoke: Macmillan, 1996).

Keith, Michael, 1993, *Race, Riots and Policing: Lore and Disorder in a Multi-racist Society* (London: UCL Press, 1993).

Kettle, M., and L. Hodges, *Uprising: The Police, the People and the Riots in Britain's Cities* (London: Pan, 1982).

Mason, D., 'After Scarman: A Note on the Concept of Institutional Racism', *New Community* X.1 (1982), pp. 38–45.

Meegan, R., 'Urban Development Corporations, Urban Entrepreneurialism and Locality: The Merseyside Development Corporation', in R. Imrie and H. Thomas (eds.), *British Urban Policy: An Evaluation of the Urban Development Corporations* (London: Sage, 1999).

Parkinson, M., and F. Bianchini, 'Liverpool: A Tale of Missed Opportunities', in M. Parkinson and F. Bianchini (eds.), *Cultural Policy and Urban Regeneration: The West European Experience* (Manchester: Manchester University Press, 1993), pp. 155–77.

Sheppard, David, *Steps Along Hope Street: My Life in Cricket, the Church and the Inner City* (London: Hodder & Stoughton, 2002).

Theokas, A., *Grounds for Review: The Garden Festival in Urban Planning and Design* (Liverpool: Liverpool University Press, 2004).

Index